Put a picture of your dog
in this box

....

Your Dog's Name

Your Dog's License Number _____

Date of Birth _____

Your Dog's Veterinarian _____

Address _____

Phone Number _____

Medications _____

Vet Emergency Number _____

Additional Emergency Numbers _____

Feeding Instructions _____

Exercise Routine _____

Favorite Treats _____

YOUR ESSENTIAL *Chihuahua* INFORMATION SHEET

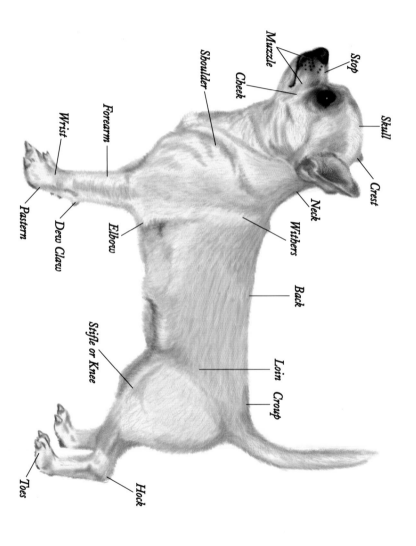

Skull

Stop

Muzzle

Cheek

Shoulder

Crest

Neck

Forearm

Wrist

Withers

Elbow

Pastern

Dew Claw

Back

Stifle or Knee

Loin

Croup

Toes

Hock

- The American Kennel Club has categorized the Chihuahua as a member of the Toy Group.

- The Chihuahua has always been known as "the smallest dog in the world," only weighing up to six pounds.

- Although there are many different theories about the Chihuahua's origin, it is stated that the breed was named after Mexico's largest northern state—Chihuahua.

- The Chihuahua was bred specifically to be a companion animal, even though it can be trained to do many useful things.

- Chihuahuas can have smooth or long coats. Any color—solid, marked, or splashed—is acceptable.

- Chihuahuas are adaptable to all spaces and make good pets in most climates and living quarters.

- Chihuahuas can be considered "lap dogs and cuddlers" because they enjoy being with their owners all the time.

- Chihuahuas require little grooming, little space and little exercise, though they do require regular attention and lots of TLC.

- Chihuahuas are excellent watchdogs. Their hearing is acute, and their bark is loud and shrill. They have been known to scare burglars and warn owners of fire and other dangers.

- The Chihuahua's popularity has increased since the breed became the star of Taco Bell commercials—"Yo quiero Taco Bell."

Consulting Editor
IAN DUNBAR PH.D., MRCVS

Featuring Photographs by
MARY BLOOM

Howell Book House
A Simon & Schuster Macmillan Company
1633 Broadway
New York, NY 10019

Macmillan Publishing books may be purchased for business or sales promotional use. For information please write: Special Markets Department, Macmillan Publishing USA, 1633 Broadway, New York, NY 10019.

The Essential Chihuahua is a revised edition of *The Chihuahua: An Owner's Guide to a Happy Healthy Pet*, first published in 1996.

Library of Congress Cataloging-in-Publication Data
       The essential Chihuahua.
          p. cm.
     Includes bibliographical references and index.
     ISBN 1-58245-021-8
     1. Chihuahua (Dog breed). I. Howell Book House.
     SF429.C45E77 1999   98-46330
     636.76—dc21
              CIP

Manufactured in the United States of America
10 9 8 7 6 5 4 3 2 1

Series Director: Michele Matrisciani
Production Team: Stephanie Mohler, Linda Quigley, Terri Sheehan
Book Design: Paul Costello
Chihuahua in cover photo, Ch. Regnier's Onth' Edge of Sunset ("Eddie"), is owned by Georgette Curran and Pat Pittore. Veterinary examination performed by Dr. Gary Selmonsky.

ARE YOU READY?!

☐ Have you prepared your home and your family for your new pet?

☐ Have you gotten the proper supplies you'll need to care for your dog?

☐ Have you found a veterinarian that you (and your dog) are comfortable with?

☐ Have you thought about how you want your dog to behave?

☐ Have you arranged your schedule to accommodate your dog's needs for exercise and attention?

No matter what stage you're at with your dog—still thinking about getting one, or he's already part of the family—this Essential guide will provide you with the practical information you need to understand and care for your canine companion. Of course you're ready—you have this book!

Chihuahua

SIGHT

The world is a much bigger place when seen through the eyes of the Chihuahua. But aside from their view, Chihuahuas, like all dogs, can detect movement at a greater distance than we can, while they can't see as well up close. They can also see better in less light, but can't distinguish many colors.

SOUND

Chihuahuas can hear about four times better than we can, and they can hear high-pitched sounds especially well.

TASTE

Chihuahuas have fewer taste buds than we do, so they're likelier to try anything—and usually do, which is why it's important for their owners to monitor their food intake. Dogs are omnivorous, which means they eat meat as well as vegetables.

TOUCH

Chihuahuas are social animals and love to be petted, groomed and played with.

SMELL

A Chihuahua's nose is his greatest sensory organ. A dog's sense of smell is so great he can follow a trail that's weeks old, detect odors diluted to one-millionth the concentration we'd need to notice them and even sniff out a person underwater!

CHAPTER ONE

Getting to Know Your Chihuahua

The Chihuahua has been consistently popular since his arrival in the United States. Why are these little dogs so beloved? The answers are numerous. Besides being cute, cuddly, charming, affectionate and bright, they are easy to manage and to take with you everywhere; they are outgoing; they are great watchdogs; and they are healthy, loyal and devoted to their owners.

Chihuahuas are known for their loyal, outgoing and affectionate natures.

LAP DOGS

Chihuahuas might be classified as "lap dogs and cuddlers." They enjoy being with you all the time, whether they are awake or sleeping. For every affectionate pat they receive, you will get double payback in love and loyalty.

Chihuahuas like to be massaged and will often roll over for a belly rub. Use caution when massaging a puppy's ears to avoid damaging the ear cartilage, which would prevent the ears from becoming erect.

The Chihuahua is happiest when he is around people, particularly his owner. He likes to cuddle, sit in your lap, be by your side and sleep in your bed. However, though you may like to be by your Chihuahua at all times, it is not safe to have him in your bed at night. Train your dog to sleep in his own bed or in a crate. This is purely a safety measure for the Chihuahua.

CHIHUAHUAS ARE LONG-LIVED

Chihuahuas live a very long time, twenty-plus years in some cases. Provide your Chihuahua with the proper medical care, a loving environment and responsible training, and you will enjoy a long and rewarding relationship with him.

Your Chihuahua will live a long and happy life with preventive health care, obedience training and lots of love.

CHIHUAHUAS ARE LOW-MAINTENANCE

Grooming Needs

The Chihuahua is considered a natural dog; there is no docking of tails and no cropping of ears. The coat is not trimmed, stripped, shaved or plucked. The dog is extremely easy to care for and maintain.

Both long coat and smooth coat Chihuahuas will shed their coats from time to time, but shedding can be kept at a minimum by appropriate grooming techniques.

Exercise Needs

Much of the Chihuahua's exercise is provided by just running around the house. Additional exercise can be achieved by providing the dog with a partially shaded run, which will give the dog a place where he can trot back and forth.

Playtime with your Chihuahua can be a form of exercise for both of you. A Chihuahua will chase a ball, catch a soft disc and retrieve small items. Whatever you use for playtime, be certain that the item is not so small that the Chihuahua could swallow it. Do not give your dog toys with eyes that could fall out, toys with strings or ribbons or toys with internal noisemakers that could be torn out and swallowed. If the toy can fit easily into the Chihuahua's mouth, it is too small and dangerous for the dog to play with.

3

Chihuahuas are great companions and long-lived dogs.

small dog is first introduced into the household of another dog of any breed, they must be supervised until the owner is certain that the various sizes are getting along well together.

CHIHUAHUAS MAKE GOOD WATCHDOGS

Chihuahuas are excellent watchdogs. Their hearing is acute, and their bark is loud and shrill. Chihuahuas have been known to scare burglars and warn owners of fire and other dangers. Because the dog's hearing is so sharp, a Chihuahua will alert the family before anyone in the household is aware of impending disaster.

Chihuahuas will not run up to a visiting houseguest and jump all over the person. They are cautious about accepting a stranger at face value and may continue to bark until requested to be quiet. Your Chihuahua will not be aggressive but will look over the guest from a distance, approaching with caution before deciding all is well.

Adaptable to All Spaces

Chihuahuas make good pets and companions in most climates and living quarters. They adapt well to most homes, whether houses, apartments or condos. (If you live in an apartment or condo, be certain that pets are allowed, especially because the Chihuahua's bark is loud and shrill.)

CHIHUAHUAS WITH OTHER DOGS

Chihuahuas usually get along well with other dog breeds, but when a

WHO SHOULD OWN A CHIHUAHUA?

The Chihuahua is ideal for older people who cannot manage larger,

4

stronger dogs and for persons and families in small living quarters. Chihuahuas make wonderful companions and can go almost anywhere, even under your seat on an airplane.

Chihuahuas are not for everyone. They are not for people who are rough—adults or children. The Chihuahua is not for you if you are worried about your furniture and rugs or if you imagine doggy odor even when there isn't any. If you worry about what mischief your puppy will get into (and a puppy will get into all kinds of mischief), you are probably not a candidate for ownership of any breed!

Chihuahuas and Children

Chihuahuas are probably not the breed to keep with a small child. A young child might accidentally fall on the dog, causing serious injury or even death to the Chihuahua. A child may think of the Chihuahua as another squeezable plaything, but a hard squeeze could seriously injure a Chihuahua. Dogs of this size should not be left with children unattended, for both the child's and the dog's sake.

CHARACTERISTICS OF THE CHIHUAHUA

affectionate

long-lived

delicate

requires minimal grooming
and exercise

has a shrill, loud bark

needs to be kept warm

When children understand that Chihuahuas are not toys, they can be best friends.

5

Children must be taught how to interact safely and humanely with dogs, particularly small ones. On the other hand, children who know how to treat a small dog like the Chihuahua properly can be wonderful companions.

SOCIALIZING YOUR CHIHUAHUA

If you do not want your Chihuahua to become aggressive, play gently with him. Otherwise, he will think that aggressive behavior is tolerated, and you'll never know when it might erupt. If the Chihuahua is taught to play in an aggressive manner or to attack, he could bite his next

Even the long-coated Chihuahuas are prone to getting cold outside.

6

playmate, be it another dog or a human being.

CHIHUAHUAS NEED TO BE KEPT WARM

Chihuahuas get cold easily, and they will shake when they feel a chill. If you live where the winters are cold, a sweater will be necessary for your Chihuahua if you will be outside for more than five minutes. A word of caution is in order for winter walks. Salt, sand and ice melters are outdoor winter hazards that will wreak havoc with your dog's feet, so be sure to wipe and clean the Chihuahua's feet after a winter walk. A dog can get frostbite, even lose toes, so be well aware of this when outside for any length of time.

CHIHUAHUA ACTIVITIES

Obedience Instruction

Even little dogs like the Chihuahua can become pests if not properly trained, so some basic obedience training is recommended. It is important that this training be gentle, positive and firm. Young puppies have a short attention span and are easily distracted.

CHAPTER TWO

Homecoming

Before bringing home your new family member, a little planning can help make the transition easier. The first decision to make is where the puppy will live. Will she have access to the entire house or be limited to certain rooms? A similar consideration applies to the yard. It is simpler to control a puppy's activities and to housetrain the puppy if she is confined to definite areas. If doors do not exist where needed, baby gates make satisfactory temporary barriers.

A dog crate is an excellent investment and is an invaluable aid in raising a puppy. It provides a safe, quiet place where a dog can sleep. Used properly, a crate helps with

PUPPY ESSENTIALS

To prepare yourself and your family for your puppy's homecoming, and to be sure your pup has what she needs, you should obtain the following:

Food and Water Bowls: One for each. We recommend stainless steel or heavy crockery—something solid but easy to clean.

Bed and/or Crate Pad: Something soft, washable and big enough for your soon-to-be-adult dog.

Crate: Make housetraining easier and provide a safe, secure den for your dog with a crate—it only looks like a cage to you!

Toys: As much fun to buy as they are for your pup to play with. Don't overwhelm your puppy with too many toys, though, especially the first few days she's home. And be sure to include something hollow you can stuff with goodies, like a Kong.

I.D. Tag: Inscribed with your name and phone number.

Collar: An adjustable buckle collar is best. Remember, your pup's going to grow fast!

Leash: Style is nice, but durability and your comfort while holding it count, too. You can't go wrong with leather for most dogs.

Grooming Supplies: The proper brushes, special shampoo, toenail clippers, a toothbrush and doggy toothpaste.

housetraining. The same crate can be used when traveling.

Before your puppy arrives, be sure to have her new home ready. Provide a bed with a washable pillow and blanket, a crate with pillow and blanket, toys for play and chewing and baby gates if you want to close off parts of the house, particularly carpeted areas.

PUPPY-PROOFING

It is definitely easier to raise a puppy than a human baby, but many of the same precautions should be taken. While puppies cannot open cabinets or stick their paws in light sockets, they can get in a lot of trouble with very little effort. Place anything that might be susceptible to puppy teeth or could be broken out of their reach. If possible, all electrical cords should be hidden or secured to floors and walls.

Puppies may also get into harmful substances. Anything that is poisonous to humans will harm a dog. Antifreeze tastes sweet and is deadly to animals. Most garden sprays, snail baits and rat poisons are toxic to dogs, so they must be kept out of reach and used with extreme caution. Another thing to

Putting your puppies in an ex-pen while they're outside will give them a safe place to play.

watch out for is the plants in the yard and in the house.

There are even things that do not bother humans that are dangerous for dogs. Such items include chocolate, onions and some salmon. The food items are potentially poisonous to dogs and should be kept away from your Chihuahua.

Yard Preparation

A small fenced-in area in your backyard will provide puppy a play area as well as a place to relieve herself. The fenced-in area should be partially shaded from the sun and other weather elements. Clean water should always be available. The run need not be large and should always be kept clean and free of feces.

Chihuahuas are house dogs and must not be left out for long periods in any kind of weather.

HOUSEHOLD DANGERS

Curious puppies and inquisitive dogs get into trouble not because they are bad, but simply because they want to investigate the world around them. It's our job to protect our dogs from harmful substances, like the following:

In the Garage
antifreeze

garden supplies, like snail and slug bait, pesticides, fertilizers, mouse and rat poisons

In the House
cleaners, especially pine oil

perfumes, colognes, aftershaves

medications, vitamins

office and craft supplies

electric cords

chicken or turkey bones

chocolate, onions

some house and garden plants, like ivy, oleander and poinsettia

Chihuahuas are natural house dogs (the majority of their days should be spent inside).

IDENTIFY YOUR DOG

It is a terrible thing to think about, but your dog could somehow, someday, get lost or stolen. For safety's sake, every dog should wear a buckle collar with an identification tag. A tag is the first thing a stranger will look for on a lost dog. Inscribe the tag with your name and phone number.

There are two ways to permanently identify your dog. The first is a tattoo, placed on the inside of your dog's thigh. The tattoo should be your social security number or your dog's AKC registration number. The second is a microchip, a rice-sized pellet that is inserted under the dog's skin at the base of the neck, between the shoulder blades. When a scanner is passed over the dog, it will beep, notifying the person that the dog has a chip. The scanner will then show a code, identifying the dog.

Chihuahua puppies have been known to squeeze through a chain-link fence or between the small openings where the gate attaches to a panel of links. Get a fence in which the links are close together, and becertain there is little, if any, space where partitions come together.

The single best preventative measure one can take to ensure that a dog is not lost or stolen is to provide her with a completely fenced yard. Check the fence periodically for digging spots or weakened structure. While most Chihuahuas are good at staying near their homes, all it takes is one unexpected occurrence for a Chihuahua to be out of her unfenced yard and in potential danger.

Make sure to include a toy or two among the supplies you buy for your puppy's homecoming.

TOYS AND ACCESSORIES

Provide your Chihuahua puppy with plenty of safe toys to keep her active and stimulated. Make sure toys do not have small parts that can be bitten off; if stuffing comes out of stuffed toys, remove them immediately. Cloth toys should be washable. Pieces of string or ribbon from

Protect your Chihuahua by providing her with proper identification (she should always wear a collar and tag).

BRINGING HOME PUPPY

- Your Chihuahua should be at least 8 weeks old before you bring her home.

- The best time of day to bring your new puppy home is in the morning. This will give you time to get acquainted and the puppy time to get acclimated to her new surroundings before bedtime. Weekends are best because the whole family will be home.

- Give the puppy freedom in a room where there is no carpet but lots of family activity. Her bed and crate can go into a corner of the room, along with a water dish and papers for "potty" training.

- No one should rush at the puppy. Keep voices soft and calm. Give your puppy time to become acclimated to the new people and strange voices.

- Keep the puppy on a routine. Establish consistent and regular periods of time for playing, eating and sleeping.

packages are not suitable playthings for your Chihuahua.

Suitable toys include stuffed chew toys, which are great for chewing and gnawing. They will keep your Chihuahua entertained and keep her teeth free of tartar.

CHAPTER THREE

To Good Health

The strongest body and soundest genetic background will not help a dog lead a healthy life unless he receives regular attention from his owner. Dogs are susceptible to infection, parasites and diseases for which they have no natural immunity. It is up to us to take preventative measures to make sure that none of these interferes with our dog's health. It may help to think of the upkeep of a dog's health in relation to the calendar. Certain things need to be done on a weekly, monthly and annual basis.

PREVENTIVE HEALTH CARE

Weekly grooming can be the single best monitor of a dog's overall

PREVENTIVE CARE PAYS

Using common sense, paying attention to your dog and working with your veterinarian, you can minimize health risks and problems. Use vet-recommended flea, tick and heartworm preventive medications; feed a nutritious diet appropriate for your dog's size, age and activity level; give your dog sufficient exercise and regular grooming; train and socialize your dog; keep current on your dog's shots; and enjoy all the years you have with your friend.

health. The actual condition of the coat and skin and the "feel" of the body can indicate good health or potential problems. Grooming will help you discover small lumps on or under the skin in the early stages before they become large enough to be seen without close examination.

You may spot fleas and ticks when brushing the coat and examining the skin. Besides harboring diseases and parasites, they can make life a nightmare for some dogs. Some Chihuahuas are allergic to even a few of fleas on their bodies. They destroy their coat and skin because of fleas.

Flea Control

Flea control is never a simple endeavor. Dogs bring fleas inside, where they lay eggs in the carpeting and furniture (anywhere your dog goes in the house). Consequently, real control is a matter of not only treating the dog but also the other environments the flea inhabits. The yard can be sprayed, and in the house, sprays and

The Chihuahua's sweet personality and small size make him an effective therapy dog.

flea bombs can be used, but there are more choices for the dog. Flea sprays are effective for one to two weeks. Dips applied to the dog's coat following a bath have equal periods of effectiveness. The disadvantage to both of these is that some dogs may have problems with the chemicals.

Flea collars prevent the fleas from traveling to your dog's head, where it's moister and more hospitable. Dog owners tend to leave flea collars on their dogs long after they've ceased to be effective. Again, some dogs may have problems with flea collars, and children should never be allowed to handle them.

Some owners opt for a product that works from the inside out. One such option is a pill (prescribed by a veterinarian) that you give to the dog on a regular basis. The chemicals in the pill course through the dog's bloodstream, and when a flea bites, the blood kills the flea.

Another available option is a product that comes in capsule form. The liquid in the capsule is applied near the dog's shoulders, close to the skin where it distributes into the skin and coat to protect against fleas and ticks. Ask your veterinarian about this non-toxic, long-lasting tick and flea preventative.

Ticks

As you examine your dog, check also for ticks that may have lodged in his skin, particularly around the ears or in the hair at the base of the ear, the

Use tweezers to remove ticks from your dog.

15

FLEAS AND TICKS

There are so many safe, effective products available now to combat fleas and ticks that—thankfully—they are less of a problem. Prevention is key, however. Ask your veterinarian about starting your puppy on a flea/tick repellant right away. With this, regular grooming and environmental controls, your dog and your home should stay pest-free. Without this attention, you risk infesting your dog and your home, and you're in for an ugly and costly battle to clear up the problem.

armpits or inguinal area. If you find a tick, which is a small insect about the size of a pencil eraser when engorged with blood, smear it with petroleum jelly. As the tick suffocates, it will back out and you can then grab it with tweezers and kill it. If the tick doesn't back out, grab it with tweezers and gently pull it out, twisting very gently. Don't just grab and pull or the tick's head may remain in the skin, causing an infection or abscess for which veterinary treatment may be required.

A word of caution: Don't use your fingers or fingernails to pull out ticks. Ticks can carry a number of diseases, including Lyme disease, Rocky Mountain spotted fever and others, all of which can be very serious.

Proper Ear Care

Another weekly job is cleaning the ears. Many times an ear problem is evident if a dog scratches his ears or shakes his head frequently. Clean ears are less likely to develop problems, and if something does occur, it will be spotted while it can be treated easily. If a dog's ears are very dirty and seem to need cleaning on a daily basis, it is a good indication that something else is going on in the ears besides ordinary dirt and the normal accumulation of earwax. A visit to the veterinarian may indicate a situation that needs special attention.

Brushing Teeth

Regular brushing of the teeth often does not seem necessary when a dog is young and spends much of his time chewing; the teeth always seem to be immaculately clean. As a dog ages, it becomes more important to brush the teeth daily.

Check your dog's teeth frequently and brush them regularly.

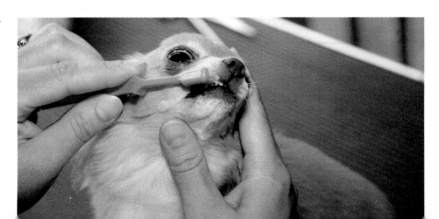

To help prolong the health of your dog's mouth, he should have his teeth cleaned twice a year at a veterinary clinic. Observing the mouth regularly, checking for the formation of abnormalities or broken teeth, can lead to early detection of oral cancer or infection.

Keeping Nails Trimmed

The nails on all feet should be kept short enough so they do not touch the ground when the dog walks.

Dogs with long nails can have difficulty walking on hard or slick surfaces. This can be especially true of older dogs. As nails grow longer, the only way the foot can compensate and retain balance is for the toes themselves to spread apart, causing the foot itself to become flattened and splayed.

Nails that are allowed to become long are also more prone to splitting.

This is painful to the dog and usually requires surgical removal of th remainder of the tail for proper hea ing to occur.

Keeping Eyes Clear

A Chihuahua's eyes rarely need special attention. A small amount of matter in the corner of the eye is normal, as is a bit of "tearing."

Chihuahuas with eyelashes that turn inward and rub against the eye itself often exhibit more tearing than normal due to the irritation to the eyes. These eyelashes can be surgically removed if it appears to be a problem, but are often ignored.

Excessive tearing can be an indication that a tear duct is blocked. This, too, can be corrected by a simple surgical procedure. Eye discharge that is thicker and mucous-like in consistency is often a sign of some

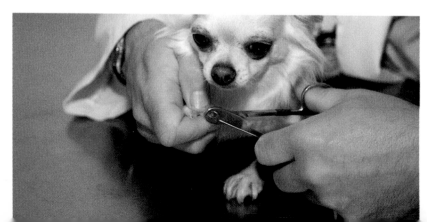

Nails that are allowed to become long are prone to splitting, which is painful to the dog.

Your Puppy's Vaccines

Vaccines are given to prevent your dog from getting an infectious disease like canine distemper or rabies. Vaccines are the ultimate preventive medicine: They're given before your dog ever gets the disease so as to protect him from the disease. That's why it is necessary for your dog to be vaccinated routinely. Puppy vaccines start at 8 weeks of age for the five-in-one DHLPP vaccine and are given every three to four weeks until the puppy is 16 months old. Your veterinarian will put your puppy on a proper schedule and should remind you when to bring in your dog for shots.

Ensure your Chihuahua's health and happiness by keeping vaccinations current.

type of eye infection or actual injury to the eye. This can be verified by a veterinarian, who will provide a topical ointment to place in the corner of the eye. Most minor eye injuries heal quickly if proper action is taken.

Vaccines

All dogs need yearly vaccinations to protect them from common deadly diseases. The DHL vaccine, which protects a dog from distemper, hepatitis and leptospirosis, is given for the first time at about 8 weeks of age, followed by one or two boosters several weeks apart. After this, a dog should be vaccinated every year throughout his life.

Since the mid-1970s, parvovirus and coronavirus have been the cause of death for thousands of dogs. Puppies and older dogs are most frequently affected by these illnesses. Fortunately, vaccines for these are now routinely given on a yearly basis in combination with the DHL shot.

Kennel cough, though rarely dangerous in a healthy dog that receives proper treatment, can be annoying. It can be picked up anywhere that large numbers of dogs congregate, such as veterinary clinics, grooming shops, boarding kennels, obedience classes and dog shows. The Bordatella vaccine, given twice a year, will protect a dog from getting most strains of kennel cough. It is often not routinely given, so it may be necessary to request it.

INTERNAL PARASITES

While the exterior part of a dog's body hosts fleas and ticks, the inside of the body is commonly inhabited by a variety of parasites. Most of these are in the worm family. Tapeworms, roundworms, whipworms, hookworms and heartworm all plague dogs. There are also several types of protozoa, mainly coccidia and giardia, that cause problems.

The common tapeworm is acquired by the dog eating infected fleas. Normally one is not aware that a healthy dog even has tapeworms. The only clues may be a dull coat, a loss of weight despite a good appetite or occasional gastrointestinal problems. Confirmation is by the presence of worm segments in the stool. These appear as small, pinkish-white, flattened rectangular-shaped pieces. When dry, they look like rice. If segments are not present, diagnosis can be made by the discovery of eggs when a stool sample is examined under a microscope. Ridding a dog temporarily of tapeworm is easy with a worming medicine prescribed by a veterinarian. Over-the-counter wormers are not effective for tapeworms and may be dangerous. Long-term tapeworm control is not possible unless the flea situation is also handled.

Ascarids are the most common roundworm (nematode) found in dogs. Adult dogs that have roundworms rarely exhibit any symptoms that would indicate the worm is in their body. These worms are cylindrical in shape and may be as long as 4 to 5 inches. They do pose a real danger to puppies, where they are usually passed from the mother through the uterus to the unborn puppies.

Diagnosis of and treament for parasites should all be done by a veterinarian.

It is wise to assume that all puppies have roundworms. In heavy infestations they will actually appear in the puppy stools, though their presence is best diagnosed by a stool sample. Treatment is easy and can begin as early as 2 weeks of age and is administered every two weeks thereafter until eggs no longer appear in a stool sample or dead worms are not found in the stool following treatment. Severely infected puppies can die from roundworm infestation. Again, the worming medication should be obtained through a veterinarian.

Hookworm is usually found in warmer climates and infestation is generally from ingestion of larvae from the ground or penetration of the skin by larvae. Hookworms can cause anemia, diarrhea and emaciation. As these worms are very tiny and not visible to the eye, their diagnosis must be made by a veterinarian.

Whipworms live in the large intestine and cause few if any symptoms. Dogs usually become infected when they ingest larvae in contaminated soil. Again, diagnosis and treatment should all be done by a veterinarian. One of the easiest ways to control these parasites is by picking up stools on a daily basis.

This will help prevent the soil from becoming infested.

The protozoa can be trickier to diagnose and treat. Coccidiosis and giardia are the most common, and primarily affect young puppies. They are generally associated with overcrowded, unsanitary conditions and can be acquired from the mother (if she is a carrier), the premises themselves (soil) or even water, especially rural puddles and streams.

The most common symptom of protozoan infection is mucous-like, blood-tinged feces. It is only with freshly collected samples that diagnosis of this condition can be made. With coccidiosis, besides diarrhea, the puppies will appear listless and lose their appetites. Puppies often harbor the protozoa and show no symptoms unless placed under stress. Consequently, many times a puppy will not become ill until he goes to his new home. Once diagnosed, treatment is quick and effective and the puppy returns to normal almost immediately.

Heartworm

The most serious of the common internal parasites is the heartworm. A dog that is bitten by a mosquito infected with the heartworm micro-filaria (larvae) will develop worms that are 6 to 12 inches long. As these worms mature they take up residence in the dog's heart.

The symptoms of heartworm may include coughing, tiring easily, difficulty breathing and weight loss. Heart failure and liver disease may eventually result. Verification of heartworm infection is done by drawing blood and screening for the microfilaria.

In areas where heartworm is a risk, it is best to place a dog on a preventative, usually a pill given once a month.

At least once a year a dog should have a full veterinary examination. The overall condition of the dog can be observed and a blood sample collected for a complete yearly screening. This way the dog's thyroid function can be tested, and the job the dog's organs are doing can be monitored. If there are any problems, this form of testing can spot trouble areas while they are easily treatable.

Proper care, regular vaccinations, periodic stool checks and preventative medications for such things as heartworm will all help ensure your dog's health.

SPAYING/NEUTERING

Spaying a female dog or neutering a male is another way to make sure they lead long and healthy lives. Females spayed at a young age have

Your Chihuahua should have a full veterinary examination at least once a year.

ADVANTAGE OF SPAYING/NEUTERING

The greatest advantage of spaying (for females) or neutering (for males) your dog is that you are guaranteed that your dog will not produce puppies. There are too many puppies already available for too few homes. There are other advantages as well.

Advantages of Spaying

No messy heats.

No "suitors" howling at your windows or waiting in your yard.

No risk of pyometra (disease of the uterus) and decreases the incidence of mammary cancer.

Advantages of Neutering

Decreased incidence of fighting, but doesn't affect the dog's personality.

Prevents roaming.

Decreased incidences of urogenital diseases.

almost no risk of developing mammary tumors or reproductive problems. Neutering a male is an excellent solution to dog aggression and also removes the chances of testicular cancer.

Female Chihuahuas usually experience their first heat cycle somewhere between 6 months and 1 year of age. Unless spayed they will continue to come into heat on a regular cycle. The length of time between heats varies, with anything from every six months to a year being normal.

There is absolutely no benefit to a female having a first season before being spayed, nor in letting her have a litter. The decision to breed any dog should never be taken lightly. The obvious considerations are whether he or she is a good physical specimen of the breed and has a sound temperament. There are several genetic problems that are common to Chihuahuas, such as molera, hydrocephalus, subluxation of the patella, heart murmur, cleft palate and hypoglycemia. Responsible breeders screen for these prior to making breeding decisions.

Finding suitable homes for puppies is another serious consideration. Due to their popularity, many people are attracted to Chihuahuas and seek puppies without realizing the drawbacks of the breed.

Owning a dog is a lifetime commitment to that animal. There are so many unwanted dogs (and yes, even unwanted Chihuahuas) that people must be absolutely sure that they are not just adding to the pet overpopulation problem. When breeding a litter of puppies, it is more likely that you will lose more than you will make, when time, effort, equipment and veterinary costs are factored in.

COMMON PROBLEMS AND FIRST AID

Not Eating or Vomiting

One of the surest signs that a Chihuahua may be ill is if he does not eat. That is why it is important to know your dog's eating habits. For most dogs, one missed meal under normal conditions is not cause for alarm, but more than that and it is time to take your dog to the veterinarian to search for reasons. The vital signs should be checked and gums examined. Normally a dog's gums are pink; if ill, they will be pale and gray.

There are many reasons why dogs vomit, and many of them are not cause for alarm. You should be concerned, however, when your dog vomits frequently over the period of a day. If the vomiting is associated

One of the surest ways to find out whether your Chihuahua is feeling well is to check that his appetite is healthy.

23

WHAT'S WRONG WITH MY DOG?

We've listed some common symptoms of health problems and their possible causes. If any of the following symptoms appear serious immediately or persist for more than 24 hours, make an appointment to see your veterinarian immediately.

CONDITION	POSSIBLE CAUSES
DIARRHEA	Intestinal upset, typically caused by eating something bad or over-eating. Can also be a viral infection, a bad case of nerves or anxiety or a parasite infection. If you see blood in the feces, get to the vet right away.
VOMITING/RETCHING	Dogs regurgitate fairly regularly (bitches for their young), whenever something upsets their stomach, or even out of excitement or anxiety. Often dogs eat grass, which, because it's indigestible in its pure form, irritates their stomachs and causes them to vomit. Getting a good look at *what* your dog vomited can better indicate what's causing it.
COUGHING	Obstruction in the throat; virus (kennel cough); roundworm infestation; congestive heart failure.
RUNNY NOSE	Because dogs don't catch colds like people, a runny nose is a sign of congestion or irritation.
LOSS OF APPETITE	Because most dogs are hearty and regular eaters, a loss of appetite can be your first and most accurate sign of a serious problem.
LOSS OF ENERGY (LETHARGY)	Any number of things could be slowing down your dog, from an infection to internal tumors to overexercise—even overeating.

with diarrhea, elevated temperature and lethargy, the cause is most likely a virus. The dog should receive supportive veterinary treatment if recovery is to proceed quickly. Vomiting that is not associated with other symptoms is often an indication of an intestinal blockage. Rocks, toys and clothing will lodge in a dog's intestine, preventing the normal passage of digested foods and liquids.

CONDITION	POSSIBLE CAUSES
STINKY BREATH	Imagine if you never brushed your teeth! Foul-smelling breath indicates plaque and tartar buildup that could possibly have caused infection. Start brushing your dog's teeth.
LIMPING	This could be caused by something as simple as a hurt or bruised pad, to something as complicated as hip dysplasia, torn ligaments or broken bones.
CONSTANT ITCHING	Probably due to fleas, mites or an allergic reaction to food or environment (your vet will need to help you determine what your dog's allergic to).
RED, INFLAMED ITCHY SPOTS	Often referred to as "hot spots," these are particularly common on coated breeds. They're caused by a bacterial infection that gets aggravated as the dog licks and bites at the spot.
BALD SPOTS	These are the result of excessive itching or biting at the skin so that the hair follicles are damaged; excessively dry skin; mange; calluses; and even infections. You need to determine what the underlying cause is.
STINKY EARS/HEADSHAKING	Take a look under your dog's ear flap. Do you see brown, waxy buildup? Clean the ears with something soft and a special cleaner, and don't use cotton swabs or go too deep into the ear canal.
UNUSUAL LUMPS	Could be fatty tissue, could be something serious (infection, trauma, tumor). Don't wait to find out.

If a blockage is suspected, the first thing to do is to get an x-ray of the stomach and intestinal region. Sometimes objects will pass on their own, but usually surgical removal of the object is necessary.

Diarrhea

Diarrhea is characterized as very loose to watery stools that a dog has difficulty controlling. It can be caused by anything as simple as changing diet, eating too much food, eating rich human food or having internal parasites.

First, try to locate the source of the problem and remove it from the dog's access. Immediate relief is usually available by giving the dog an intestinal relief medication, such as Kaopectate or Pepto-Bismol. Use the same amount per weight as for humans. Take the dog off his food for a day to allow the intestines to rest, then feed meals of cooked rice with bland ingredients added. Gradually add the dog's regular food back into his diet.

If diarrhea is bloody or has a more offensive odor than might be expected and is combined with vomiting and fever, it is most likely a virus and requires immediate veterinary attention. If worms are suspected as the cause, a stool sample should be examined by a veterinarian and treatment to rid the dog of the parasite should follow when the dog is back to normal. If allergies are suspected, a series of tests can be given to find the cause. This

is especially likely, if after recovery and no other evidence of a cause exists, a dog returns to his former diet and the diarrhea recurs.

Dehydration

To test your dog for dehydration, take some skin between your thumb and forefinger and lift the skin upward gently. If the skin does not go back to its original position immediately, it is possible that your Chihuahua is suffering from dehydration. Consult your veterinarian immediately.

Poisoning

Vomiting, breathing with difficulty, diarrhea, cries of pain and abnormal body or breath odor are all signs that your pet may have ingested some poisonous substance. Poisons can also be inhaled, absorbed through the skin or injected into the skin, as in the case of a snakebite. Poisons require professional help without delay!

Broken Bones

If your dog breaks a bone, immobilize the limb very carefully, and seek veterinary help right away.

Make a temporary splint by wrapping the leg in firm casing, then bandaging it.

Scratches and Cuts

For minor skin problems, many oint-ments suitable for a baby work well on a Chihuahua.

Heatstroke

Heatstroke can quickly lead to death. Never leave your dog in a car, even with the windows open, even on a cloudy day with the car under the shade of a tree. Heat builds up quickly; your dog could die in a matter of minutes. Do not leave your Chi-huahua outside on a hot day, especi-ally if no shade or water is provided.

Heatstroke symptoms include collapse, high fever, diarrhea, vomit-ing, excessive panting and grayish lips. If you notice these symptoms, you need to cool the animal imme-diately. Try to reduce the body tem-perature with towels soaked in cold water; massage the body and legs very gently. Fanning the dog may help. If the dog will drink cool water, let him. If he will not drink, wipe the inside of his mouth with cool water. Get the dog to the nearest veterinary hospital. Do not delay!

Bee Stings

Bee stings are painful and may cause an allergic reaction. Symptoms may

Some of the many household substances harm-ful to your dog.

be swelling around the bite and difficulty breathing. Severe allergic reaction could lead to death. If a stinger is present, remove it. Clean the bitten area thoroughly with al-cohol; apply a cold compress to reduce swelling and itching and an anti-inflammatory ointment or cream medication. Seek medical help.

Choking

Puppies are curious creatures and will naturally chew anything they can get into their mouths, be it a bone, a twig, stones, tiny toys, string or any number of things. These can get

Applying abdo-minal thrusts can save a choking dog.

27

caught in the teeth or, worse, lodged in the throat and may finally rest in the stomach or intestines.

Symptoms may be drooling, pawing at the mouth, gagging, difficulty breathing, blue tongue or mouth, difficulty swallowing and bloody vomit. If the foreign object can be seen and you can remove it easily, do so. If you can't remove it yourself, use the Heimlich maneuver. Place your dog on his side and, using both hands palms down, apply quick thrusts to the abdomen, just below the dog's last rib. If your dog won't lie down, grasp either side of the end of the rib cage and squeeze in short thrusts. Make a sharp enough movement to cause the air in the lungs to force the object out. If the cause cannot be found or removed, then professional help is needed.

Bleeding

For open wounds, try to stop the bleeding by applying pressure to the wound for five minutes using a sterile bandage. If bleeding has not stopped after this time, continue the pressure. Do not remove the pad if it sticks to the wound because more serious injury could result. Just place a new sterile bandage over the first,

and apply a little more pressure to stop the bleeding. This procedure will usually be successful. Take the dog to the medical center for treatment especially if the bleeding cannot be controlled rapidly.

If bleeding cannot be stopped with pressure, try pressing on the upper inside of the front leg, on the upper inside of the rear leg or on the underside of the tail at its base, depending on where the dog is bleeding. Do not attempt to stop the bleeding with a tourniquet unless the bleeding is profuse and cannot be stopped any other way. A tourniquet must be tight; consequently, it cannot be left on for a long time because it will stop the circulation. It could be more dangerous than the bleeding!

Burns

Do not put creams or oils on a burn. Cool water can be used to carefully wash the burn area. Transport to the veterinary clinic immediately.

PROBLEMS PARTICULAR TO THE CHIHUAHUA

The Chihuahua is fortunate in that the breed does not have a great many defects or problems. Breeders work hard to eliminate the defects that do exist, but no matter how diligent a breeder is, problems may creep in once in a while.

Molera (Fontanel)

The molera, also referred to as the fontanel, is a soft spot at the top of the skull, very similar to a baby's soft spot. Sometimes it will disappear completely, though usually it does not. In a puppy, the molera is enlarged and will gradually grow smaller as the puppy matures, though it may never completely disappear. If it remains about the size of a dime,

The Chihuahua is fortunate in that the breed does not have a great many defects or problems.

When choosing your puppy, be sure to ask the breeder about the history of disease in the puppy's lineage.

there is nothing to worry about; just avoid heavy-handedness while patting the skull. If the molera is excessively large on the skull of an adult or a puppy, there may possibly be a health problem related to hydrocephalus especially if the extraordinarily large molera is accompanied by other symptoms.

The molera is not a defect in the breed, but a unique characteristic of the breed. As far we know, the Chihuahua is the only breed that may have this trait and still be a perfectly healthy dog. According to the breed standard, the Chihuahua may or may not have a molera; 80 percent to 90 percent of Chihuahuas do.

Because of their slightly protruding eyes, Chihuahuas can be prone to eye injuries.

Hydrocephalus

This ailment is sometimes referred to as water on the brain. The head may be excessively large, usually due to swelling. Other symptoms are unsteadiness when walking, frequent falling, eyes that look in opposite directions (also known as east-west eyes), lots of white showing around the eyeballs and seizures. Puppies or adults with these symptoms usually do not live long. If the Chihuahua shows all the signs of hydrocephalus, it is more humane to have the dog "put to sleep" than to have him go through a limited life span in this painful condition.

Subluxation of the Patella

This condition is also known as slipping stifles (kneecaps). With this problem, the kneecap does not glide smoothly along the groove, but slips out from time to time. In a severe case, surgery can help correct the problem. In mild cases, surgery is not recommended because the dog will be able to live a relatively normal life, though he may not be an active jumper. Arthritis may develop as the dog ages, but it is apt to occur even in a dog with perfectly normal kneecaps. Subluxation of

the patella appears in many small breeds.

Heart Murmur

Occasionally, a Chihuahua will develop a heart murmur, but just as in humans, the dog can usually lead a normal existence and a long life. This is not a very common problem in the breed.

Cleft Palate

Once in a while, a dog is born with a hole in the roof of the mouth, called a cleft palate. Dogs with this problem are unable to eat, so when this condition is discovered in a young puppy, the dog should be humanely euthanized.

Hypoglycemia

Low blood sugar is known as hypoglycemia. It will usually occur in very young puppies. Quite often a puppy will outgrow the condition and live a perfectly normal life. The symptoms are rigidity or limpness, unsteady gait and seizures that may turn to unconsciousness. Sometimes, the symptoms last only a few seconds, though they may last as long as several minutes. Try to get some kind of sugar and water

mixture into the animal's mouth, but take care that the puppy does not choke on the substance. It is imperative that immediate veterinary help be sought. Although not a common problem in the breed, it is mentioned here so that you will recognize the symptoms and take immediate corrective action.

Eye Injuries

Because of their slightly protruding eyes, Chihuahuas can be prone to eye injuries. If your Chihuahua injures an eye, flush it out for several minutes using water or a saline solution. This treatment may be sufficient, but if not, transport the dog to a hospital.

Anesthesia

Breeders of small dogs always worry about shock or even death from

Squeeze eye ointment into the lower lid.

31

anesthesia. It is highly recommended that anesthesia be given only when necessary. Because of the potential harmful effects of anesthesia, small dog owners need to be especially diligent about practicing good dental hygiene on their Chihuahuas, thus making teeth cleaning under anesthesia unnecessary.

To begin with, select a veterinarian or animal clinic with modern equipment and a staff that is knowledgeable about the latest methods of administering anesthesia.

Impacted Anal Glands

Impacted anal glands may be a problem. If you see your Chihuahua constantly scooting along the ground on his rear end or trying to lick himself around the anus, the anal glands may be impacted. Have your veterinarian show you how to empty these

sacs; otherwise, a trip to the veterinarian may be needed about every six months to take care of this problem. If the anal sacs are not emptied regularly, infection may occur and surgery may be required.

GIVING MEDICATION

When a dog has been diagnosed with a problem that requires medication, it is usually in the form of a pill or liquid. Because it is essential for a dog to have the entire pill or capsule in order for the dosage to be effective, it's necessary to actually give the dog the pill rather than mix it in his food or wrap it in meat, which can be chewed up and spit out. Open your dog's mouth and place the pill on the back of the middle of his tongue. Then hold his head up with his mouth held shut and stoke his throat. When the dog swallows, you can let go.

Liquid medication is most easily given in a syringe. These are usually marked so the amount is accurately measured. Hold the dog's head upward at about 45 degrees, open the mouth slightly and place the end of the syringe in the area in the back of the mouth between the cheek and rear molars. Hold

To give a pill, open the mouth wide, then drop it in the back of the throat.

your dog's mouth shut until he swallows.

If your dog needs eye medication, apply it by pulling down the lower eyelid and placing the ointment on the inside of the lid. Then close the eye and gently disperse the solution around the eye. Eye drops can be placed directly on the eye. Giving ear medicine is similar to cleaning the ears. The drops are placed in the canal and the ear is then massaged.

FIRST AID AND EMERGENCIES

While we never plan on emergencies happening, we can be partially prepared by knowing which veterinary clinics are open if something occurs at night or on the weekend. Telephone numbers should be posted so they can be easily located.

First-aid measures can be taken to help ensure that your dog gets to a veterinarian in time for treatment to be effective.

Anytime a dog is in extreme pain, even the most docile one may bite if touched. As a precaution, the dog's mouth should be restrained with a muzzle. A rope, pair of pantyhose or strip of cloth about 2 feet long all work in a pinch.

POISONING ALERT

If your dog has ingested a potentially poisonous substance, waste no time. Call the National Animal Poison Control Center hot line:

(800) 548-2423 ($30 per case) or

(900) 680-0000 ($20 first five minutes; $2.95 each additional minute)

First, tie a loose knot that has an opening large enough to easily fit around the dog's nose. Once it is on, tighten the knot on the top of the muzzle. Then bring the two ends down and tie another knot underneath the dog's chin. Finally, pull the ends behind the head and tie a knot below the ears. Don't do this if there is an injury to the head or the dog requires artificial respiration.

Artificial Respiration

Artificial respiration is necessary if breathing has stopped. Situations that may cause a state of unconsciousness include drowning, choking, electric shock or even shock itself. If you've taken a course in human CPR, you will discover that similar methods are used on dogs. The first thing to do is check the

33

WHEN TO CALL THE VETERINARIAN

In any emergency situation, you should call your veterinarian immediately. Try to stay calm when you call, and give the vet or the assistant as much information as possible before you leave for the clinic. That way, the staff will be able to take immediate, specific action when you arrive. Emergencies include:

- Shock
- Dehydration
- Abdominal pain
- Burns
- Fits
- Unconsciousness
- Paralysis
- Broken bones

Call your veterinarian if you suspect any health troubles.

mouth and air passages for any object that might obstruct breathing. If you find nothing, or when they are cleared, hold the dog's mouth while covering the nose completely with your mouth. Very gently exhale into the dog's nose. This should be done at between ten to twelve breaths per minute.

If the heart has stopped beating, place the dog on his right side and place the palm of your hand on the rib cage just behind the elbows. Press down six times and then wait five seconds and repeat. This should be done in conjunction with artificial respiration, so it will require two people. Artificial respiration should be continued until the dog breathes on his own or the heart beats. Heart massage should continue until the heart beats on its own or no beat is felt for five minutes.

Shock

Whenever a dog is injured or is seriously ill, the odds are good that he will go into a state of shock. A dog in shock will be listless, weak and cold to the touch. His gums will be pale. If not treated, a dog will die from shock, even if the illness or injuries themselves are not fatal. The conditions of the dog should continue to be treated, but the dog should be kept as comfortable as possible. A blanket can help keep the dog warm. A dog in shock needs immediate veterinary care.

Severe Bleeding

When severe bleeding from a cut occurs, the area should be covered

*A healthy
Chihuahua
is a happy
Chihuahua.*

with bandaging material or a clean cloth and should have pressure applied to it. If it appears that an artery is involved and the wound is on a limb, then a tourniquet should be applied. This can be made of a piece of cloth, gauze or sock if nothing else is available. It should be tied above the wound and checked every few minutes to make sure it is not so tight that circulation to the rest of the limb is cut off.

CHAPTER FOUR

Positively Nutritious

The nutritional needs of a dog will change throughout her lifetime. It is necessary to be aware of these changes not only for proper initial growth to occur, but also so your dog can lead a healthy life for many years.

Before bringing your puppy home, ask the breeder for the puppy's feeding schedule and information about what and how much she is used to eating. Maintain this regimen for at least the first few days before gradually changing to a schedule that is more in line with the family's lifestyle. The breeder may supply you with a small quantity of the food the puppy has been eating. Use this or have your own supply of the same food ready when you bring home your puppy.

After the puppy has been with you for three days and has become acclimated to her new environment, you can begin a gradual food change. Add a portion of the new food to the usual food. Add a little more of the new food each day until it has entirely replaced the previous diet. This gradual change will prevent an upset stomach and diarrhea. The total amount of food to be fed at each meal will remain the same at this stage of the puppy's life.

LIFE-STAGE FEEDING

Puppies and adolescent dogs require a much higher intake of protein, calories and nutrients than adult dogs due to the demands of their

GROWTH STAGE FOODS

Once upon a time, there was puppy food and there was adult dog food. Now there are foods for puppies, young adults/active dogs, less-active dogs and senior citizens. What's the difference between these foods? They vary by the amounts of nutrients they provide for the dog's growth stage/activity level.

Less active dogs don't need as much protein or fat as growing, active dogs; senior dogs don't need some of the nutrients vital to puppies. By feeding a high-quality food that's appropriate for your dog's age and activity level, you're benefiting your dog and yourself. Feed too much protein to a couch potato and she'll have energy to spare, which means a few more trips around the block will be needed to burn it off. Feed an adult diet to a puppy, and risk growth and development abnormalities that could affect her for a lifetime.

37

Puppies require a high intake of protein, calories and nutrients due to their rapidly developing bodies.

How Many Meals a Day?

Individual dogs vary in how much they should eat to maintain a desired body weight—not too fat, but not too thin. Puppies need several meals a day, while older dogs may need only one. Determine how much food keeps your adult dog looking and feeling her best. Then decide how many meals you want to feed with that amount. Like us, most dogs love to eat, and offering two meals a day is more enjoyable for them. If you're worried about overfeeding, make sure you measure correctly and abstain from adding tidbits to the meals.

Whether you feed one or two meals, only leave your dog's food out for the amount of time it takes her to eat it—ten minutes, for example. Freefeeding (when food is available any time) and leisurely meals encourage picky eating. Don't worry if your dog doesn't finish all her dinner in the allotted time. She'll learn she should.

rapidly developing bodies. Most commercial brands of dry kibble meet these requirements and are well balanced for proper growth. The majority of puppy foods now available are so carefully planned that it is unwise to attempt to add anything other than water to them.

The major ingredients of most dry dog foods are chicken, beef or lamb by-products and corn, wheat or rice. The higher the meat content, the higher the protein percentage, palatability and digestibility of the food. Protein percentages in puppy food are usually between 25 and 30 percent. There are many advantages of dry foods over semimoist and canned dog foods for puppies and normal, healthy adult Chihuahuas.

It is best to feed meals that are primarily dry food because the chewing action involved in eating a dry

You'll know your Chihuahua's getting what she needs in her diet if her skin and coat look good, her eyes are shiny and she's full of energy, like these playful pups.

food is better for the health of the teeth and gums. Dry food is also less expensive than canned food of equal quality.

Dogs whose diets are based on canned or soft foods have a greater likelihood of developing calcium deposits and gum disease. Canned or semimoist foods do serve certain functions, however. As a supplement to dry dog food, in small portions, canned or semimoist foods can be useful to stimulate appetites and aid in weight gain. But unless very special conditions exist they are not the best way for a dog to meet her food needs.

YOUR PUPPY'S MEAL PLAN

Your puppy will be on four meals a day until you see that she's leaving food in the dish. At this point, she no longer needs four meals; it's now time to switch to three meals at equal intervals.

Your puppy will let you know when it is time to go to two meals a day, spaced about ten to twelve hours apart. Again, she will begin to leave food in the bowl on the three-meals-per-day schedule. Increase the portions given at each meal when you switch to two meals a day. It will take

HOW TO READ THE DOG FOOD LABEL

With so many choices on the market, how can you be sure you are feeding the right food for your dog? The information is all there on the label—if you know what you're looking for.

Look for the nutritional claim right up top. Is the food "100% nutritionally complete"? If so, it's for nearly all life stages; "growth and maintenance," on the other hand, is for early development; puppy foods are marked as such, as are foods for senior dogs.

Ingredients are listed in descending order by weight. The first three or four ingredients will tell you the bulk of what the food contains. Look for the highest-quality ingredients, like meats and grains, to be among them.

The Guaranteed Analysis tells you what levels of protein, fat, fiber and moisture are in the food, in that order. While these numbers are meaningful, they won't tell you much about the quality of the food. Nutritional value is in the dry matter, not the moisture content.

In many ways, seeing is believing. If your dog has bright eyes, a shiny coat, a good appetite and a good energy level, chances are her diet's fine. Your dog's breeder and your veterinarian are good sources of advice if you're still confused.

a little trial and error to determine how much food you should offer at

Your full-grown Chihuahua should be fed twice a day, about every twelve hours.

TO SUPPLEMENT OR NOT TO SUPPLEMENT

If you're feeding your dog a diet that's correct for her developmental stage and she's alert, healthy-looking and neither over- nor underweight, you don't need to add supplements. These include table scraps as well as vitamins and minerals. In fact, unless you are a nutrition expert, using food supplements can actually hurt a growing puppy. For example, mixing too much calcium into your dog's food can lead to musculoskeletal disorders. Educating yourself about the quantity of vitamins your dog needs to be healthy will help you determine what needs to be supplemented. If you have any concerns about the nutritional quality of the food you're feeding, discuss them with your veterinarian.

each meal. Again, the dog should be fed at the same time each day.

The puppy should receive a minimum of one-quarter cup of food at each meal (given four times a day). If she still appears to be hungry, then increase the amount given at each meal. Each puppy is an individual, and just as members of your family eat different-sized portions, so will the individual Chihuahua.

When your Chihuahua is placed on a two-meals-per-day regimen, one meal should consist of dry food soaked in hot water for five minutes (be sure it has cooled before feeding). Mix the moistened food with a rounded tablespoon, minimum, of canned food. The canned food should also be manufactured by a well-known dog food company. Check the ingredients rather than the price, and do not skimp on quality.

The second meal of the day should consist of dry food only. As the dog crunches up the food, the dry pieces will scrape against the teeth, helping keep them clean.

Fresh, clean water must be available at all times. The water dish should be cleaned and replenished more than once a day. Dogs who eat primarily dry kibble will probably drink more water. Thoroughly clean

and rinse the water dish every day.
Do not use any disinfectant to wash
your Chihuahua's dishes.

For an occasional treat, offer tiny
dog biscuits. These help keep your
dog's teeth clean. One or two a day
is fine, but do not substitute these
biscuits for regular food or you may
inadvertently encourage finicky eating habits in your dog.

WEIGHT PROBLEMS

If your pet has become a couch potato, the place to cut back is probably
in the amount of fat and calories
that the dog is consuming. If your
Chihuahua is weighing in at 12
pounds and is only 7 inches tall, she
would be placed in the obese cate-
gory! Carrying excess weight is bad
for the dog's heart, her limbs and her
life expectancy. If you cannot easily
feel the ribs of the Chihuahua, she
is most likely overweight.

Some older dogs have the opposite problem; these dogs are underweight. If the older dog is not
suffering from a medical problem but
is still underweight, try a premium
dog food that is packed with nutrients. Discuss this with your veterinarian. The condition and general
health of the Chihuahua must be

FOOD ALLERGIES

If your puppy or dog seems to itch all the time
for no apparent reason, she could be allergic
to one or more ingredients in her food. This
is not uncommon, and it's why many foods
contain lamb and rice instead of beef, wheat or
soy. Have your dog tested by your veterinarian,
and be patient while you strive to identify and
eliminate the allergens from your dog's food
(or environment).

considered before any dietary changes
for the older dog are made.

FORBIDDEN FOODS

Dogs love chocolate, but under no
circumstances should your Chihuahua get even one small tidbit of it.
Dogs cannot digest chocolate the
way we can, although they love the
taste just as much as we do. Some
dogs have perished from an overdose
of chocolate.

Do not feed the Chihuahua from
your plate while you are dining.
Table feeding will turn the dog
into a table pest, which is annoying to you and embarrassing when
you have company. This practice will
also turn your Chihuahua into a
finicky eater.

41

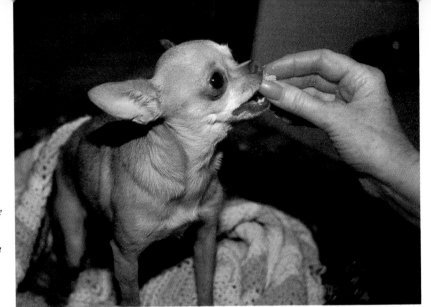

Keep dinner scraps and doggie treats to a minimum; these extra calories can lead to unhealthy weight gain.

THE PICKY EATER

Allow your Chihuahua only ten minutes to eat her meal. If she has not finished in that time, take away the food and dispose of it. A dog that lingers over food for a half hour or more will tend to become a picky eater. There's no need to feel sorry for your dog. A healthy dog will eat before she starves.

Occasionally, a dog will "go off her feed" or, in other words, will not want to eat anything for a day or so. If the dog appears to be normal in all other respects, then she is probably all right. A visit to the veterinarian is warranted if the dog shows signs of illness or does not eat for three days.

CHAPTER FIVE

Putting on the Dog

Good grooming techniques and a faithful grooming program will help keep your Chihuahua clean and in good physical condition.

Grooming should begin while a dog is a puppy and should become routine. Some breeders clip puppy nails weekly until they go to their new homes. This teaches the puppy to accept having his nails clipped. Some breeders also use a fine-toothed comb daily to remove dirt from the coats. Mouths and baby teeth are checked to see how bites are developing, and ears are observed for cleanliness. All of these preliminary steps taken by the breeder will help make grooming easier for the new owner as long as the process is continued.

GETTING STARTED

For starters, one will need a natural bristle brush for the body coat, and a hard rubber comb for the ear fringe, pants and leg fringes. The tail plume

GROOMING TOOLS

- Pin brush
- Slicker brush
- Flea comb
- Towel
- Mat rake
- Grooming glove
- Scissors
- Nail clippers
- Tooth-cleaning equipment
- Shampoo
- Conditioner
- Clippers

will take both a brush and a hard rubber comb. When a puppy is young, it is a good idea to brush and/or comb him daily. If a puppy is not already used to having his nails clipped, it is best to start this now rather than waiting and battling an adult dog. Human nail clippers can be used on puppies until they are about 3 months old. These make it easier to remove just the tips of tiny nails. Be sure not to clip the dew-claws if these have not been removed.

Check your Chihuahua's ears regularly, and even if they do not look dirty, get him used to having a cotton swab soaked in a little ear cleaner run around the inside of the ear. Lift up your dog's lips and inspect the

Cleaning your dog's ears is simple. Just run a moistened cotton ball along the inside ear flap and avoid cleaning into the ear canal.

mouth. Your puppy will become used to being examined and having sensitive parts of his body handled, and you will learn what is normal for your dog, making it easier to spot potential problems before they require more serious attention.

BRUSHING

Whether your Chihuahua is a long coat or a smooth coat, it is still necessary to have frequent brushings.

A thorough brushing three times a week is absolutely necessary; daily brushing is even better. Frequent brushing means less hair around the house, and your Chihuahua will be cleaner and need fewer baths.

While going through the coat, look for mats; these are clumps of fine hair stuck together. If mats are a problem, particularly the very fine hairs of the ear fringe, you are not brushing often enough, or the dog is dirty.

A Chihuahua's coat grows in cycles. It will grow for a while, then stop, then dry out, and from there it will shed. It takes about 125 to 135 days to complete the cycle, on average, but this time frame will vary. Shedding takes place, usually in the spring, when dogs get rid of the

Frequently brushing your Chihuahua is especially important during heavy shedding periods.

winter coat, but because Chihuahuas are house dogs, they probably will not have a heavier winter coat, so shedding may occur at any time, depending on whether they keep close to the heat or air-conditioner ducts.

DON'T FORGET NAILS

Trimming nails is essential for the well-being of your dog's feet. Normally, nails should be trimmed every two weeks or when the nails start to touch the floor. This is noticeable as a clicking sound when the dog walks on hard surfaces.

If clipping nails is a scary proposition for you, most groomers and

45

QUICK AND PAINLESS NAIL CLIPPING

This is possible if you make a habit out of handling your dog's feet and giving your dog treats when you do. When it's time to clip nails, go through the same routine, but take your clippers and snip off just the ends of the nail—clip too far down and you'll cut into the "quick," the nerve center, hurting your dog and causing the nail to bleed. Clip two nails at a time while you're getting your dog used to the procedure, and you'll soon be doing all four feet quickly and easily.

veterinary clinics will take care of it for a small fee.

CARING FOR EARS AND TEETH

Your Chihuahua's ears will need weekly cleaning. Even if they do not

appear dirty, frequent care will prevent ear problems. Ear-cleaning solutions are available in pet stores. Place several drops in each ear and massage the ears for half a minute. This way the solution can penetrate the greasy dirt. Let the dog shake his head to loosen the dirt. To actually remove the dirt, use cotton swabs or cotton balls. Clean the exterior areas of the inside of the ear, getting into the nooks and crannies of the outer ear. A need for more frequent cleanings may require veterinary attention.

We rarely think about the cleanliness of our dog's teeth, leaving that to the natural cleansing action of chewing. However, dogs develop gum disease and tooth degeneration just like humans. We can help counter this progression by brushing the teeth regularly. Canine toothbrushes and toothpastes are available and can be used regularly.

Regularly brushing your Chihuahua's teeth will help prevent tooth and gum disease.

CHAPTER SIX

Measuring Up

WHAT IS A BREED STANDARD?

A breed standard (a detailed description of an individual breed) is meant to portray the ideal specimen of that breed. This includes ideal structure, temperament, gait and type (all aspects of the dog). Because the standard describes an ideal specimen, it isn't based on any particular dog. It is a concept against which judges compare actual dogs and breeders strive to produce dogs. At a dog show, the dog that wins is the one that comes closest, in the judge's opinion, to the standard for her breed.

Chihuahuas, according to the official standard written by the Chihuahua Club of America and approved by

47

the American Kennel Club (AKC), are "graceful, alert, swift-moving, compact, and with a saucy expression." This brief description of the breed is excellent, but it only begins to touch on the essence of the Chihuahua. This chapter will attempt to explicate the appearance and personality of the breed, according to the AKC standard. It is important to keep in mind when reading the standard

THE AMERICAN KENNEL CLUB

Familiarly referred to as "the AKC," the American Kennel Club is a nonprofit organization devoted to the advancement of purebred dogs. The AKC maintains a registry of recognized breeds and adopts and enforces rules for dog events including shows, obedience trials, field trials, hunting tests, lure coursing, herding, earth-dog trials, agility and the Canine Good Citizen program. It is a club of clubs, established in 1884 and composed, today, of over 500 autonomous dog clubs throughout the United States. Each club is represented by a delegate; the delegates make up the legislative body of the AKC, voting on rules and electing directors. The American Kennel Club maintains the Stud Book, the record of every dog ever registered with the AKC, and publishes a variety of materials on purebred dogs, including a monthly magazine, books and numerous educational pamphlets. For more information, contact the AKC at the address listed in Chapter 9, "Resources."

and trying to match one's own Chihuahua to it that the standard describes an ideal Chihuahua, and some sections are geared toward a show interpretation.

What follow are descriptions of the ideal Chihuahua. Excerpts from the breed standard appear in italics,

and are followed by an explanation of their statements.

SIZE

A well-balanced little dog not to exceed 6 pounds.

The Chihuahua has always been known as "the smallest dog in the world!" It was true when the breed first arrived in the United States; it is still true today. The Chihuahua is classified as a Toy breed and is shown in the Toy Group at AKC events. Chihuahuas can range in weight up to 6 pounds. No matter the size within that range, the physical characteristics remain the same.

HEAD

A well rounded "apple dome" skull, with or without molera.
Expression—Saucy.

Both varieties of the Chihuahua, smooth coat and long coat, have large, well-rounded "apple dome" skulls. The molera is a slight indentation on the top of the skull, like the soft spot on a baby's head. The indentation is not visible but can be felt with a gentle touch. Although care should be taken not to press on this spot, there should be little concern about this soft area.

Adult Chihuahuas may range in weight up to 6 pounds.

EARS

Large, erect type ears, held more upright when alert, but flaring to the sides at a 45 degree angle when in repose, giving breadth between the ears.

Chihuahua ears are quite large and set somewhat low on the head. When the ears are at rest, they point to about ten o'clock and two o'clock. When alert, they are carried closer to eleven o'clock and one o'clock, or slightly higher. Ears that are carried as high as twelve o'clock would be considered too high and would make the dog look rabbitlike.

WHAT IS A BREED STANDARD?

A breed standard—a detailed description of an individual breed—is meant to portray the ideal specimen of that breed. This includes ideal structure, temperament, gait, type—all aspects of the dog. Because the standard describes an ideal specimen, it isn't based on any particular dog. It is a concept against which judges compare actual dogs and breeders strive to produce dogs. At a dog show, the dog that wins is the one that comes closest, in the judge's opinion, to the standard for its breed. Breed standards are written by the breed parent clubs, the national organizations formed to oversee the well-being of the breed. They are voted on and approved by the members of the parent clubs.

EYES

Full, but not protruding, balanced, well set apart—luminous dark or luminous ruby.

Eyes are somewhat large and full but not protruding. They should never bulge like the eyes of some of the very short-nosed Toy breeds. Although eye color is usually dark, lighter eyes are permissible in light-colored dogs. The ruby eye has a reddish cast to its coloring and is generally found only on very deep red-colored dogs.

This Chihua-hua puppy is already exhi-biting a saucy expression.

BITE

Level or scissors.

The bite may be level, with the edges of the upper and lower teeth just touching, or a scissors, with the upper teeth over and slightly cover-ing the top of the bottom teeth, like a pair of scissors.

MUZZLE

Moderately short, slightly pointed. Cheeks and jaws lean.

The muzzle, sometimes called the snout, is moderately short and slightly pointed. An excessively short muzzle is not desirable because the teeth may become crowded or breath-ing problems may occur.

Although the standard does not mention a stop (the indentation lo-cated between the eyes separating the top skull from muzzle), the Chi-huahua should have a medium stop. It would be impossible to have the round, apple-domed skull and mod-erately short muzzle without at least a medium stop.

NOSE

Self-colored in blond types, or black. In moles, blues, and chocolates, they are self-colored. In blonde types, pink nose permissible.

The nose is very dark in dark-colored dogs, and lighter in light-colored dogs. Blue dogs will have a blue nose, and chocolates a chocolate or lighter brown nose. A pink nose is permissible in very light-colored dogs, such as white or cream. Less desirable is the nose that has a light streak running down the middle. This coloration is sometimes referred to as a winter nose, and the light streak may disappear during the summer.

BODY

Neck

Slightly arched, gracefully sloping into lean shoulders.

Topline

Level.

Body

Ribs rounded and well sprung (but not too much "barrel shaped").

The Chihuahua neck has a slight arch to it, and the topline is level. Although the ribs are rounded, they should not be fully rounded like a barrel. The body should be off-square in both males and females. Although

the male's may be a little shorter than the female's, the male's body should still be off-square. The Chihuahua must not appear to be square in shape when viewed from a profile.

TAIL

Moderately long, carried sickle either up or out, or in a loop over the back with just the tip touching the back.

Tails are moderately long and carried in any one of three positions: in a sickle out from the body, in a sickle upright or in a loop over the back. The tail should never be carried between the legs, which would indicate fright, chilliness, shyness, illness or even a broken tail.

Regardless of your Chihuahua's rating in terms of the breed standard, a healthy dog with a great temperament will make a wonderful pet.

51

FEET

A small dainty foot with toes well split up but not spread, pads cushioned.

Feet are small and dainty, neither round nor pointed, but halfway between. The toes are noticeably separated, but should not be wide apart.

CHIHUAHUA COLORS

Color

Any color—Solid, marked or splashed.

Chihuahuas come in all colors, including white, fawn, red, black and sable, to name just a few. They may also be any combination of those colors, as well as various shades from very light to very dark. There is even a blue, and blue coupled with other colors, such as tan or white, but the blue is not as common as those previously mentioned.

COAT

In the smooth coats, the coat should be of soft texture, close and glossy. Coat placed well over body with ruff on neck preferred, and more scanty over head and ears. In long coats the coat should be of a soft texture, either flat or slightly curly, with undercoat preferred.

Chihuahuas may be seen in any color or combination of colors.

There are two varieties of Chihuahua: smooth coat and long coat. Except for coat, there is no difference between the two. All breed characteristics are the same for the two varieties.

The Smooth Chihuahua

The smooth coat Chihuahua has a very short and close-to-the-body coat, and may have an undercoat. An undercoat is a layer of fur under the top, or outer, coat. There may be sparser coat (approaching baldness) on the chest, the temples of the head, the ears and the under-belly if no undercoat is present.

The tail of the smooth coat should be covered with furry hair. The smooth coat should also have a slight ruff around the neck, but no fringes or plume like the long coat variety. If the smooth coat Chihuahua does not have an undercoat, she will not have a full ruff around the neck; neither will she have a tail that is heavily coated.

The Long Coat Chihuahua

The long coat Chihuahua has a slightly longer body coat, about 1 to 1½ inches in length, with a definite undercoat. An undercoat is an absolute necessity in the long coat variety. The long coat Chihuahua has fringe, sometimes called feathering, around the edges of the ears; a ruff around the neck; wisps of hair extending along the back of each leg; long hair, called pants, at the buttocks; and long, flowing hair, called a plume, on the tail. These fringes and plume are called furnishings. If the body coat is thick and full, the furnishings are usually more abundant. The standard neither indicates the amount or length of furnishings required nor

The long coat Chihuahua has a heavier coat as well as fringes and tail plume.

53

Your Chihuahua should look energetic, vivacious and light-hearted.

mentions the length or thickness of the body coat. Aside from the heavier coat, fringes and tail plume, the long coat Chihuahua should resemble and have the same physical characteristics and conformation as a smooth coat.

No matter how heavy a coat a smooth coat Chihuahua has, she is not considered a long coat because she will have no furnishings at the edges of the ears or a plume on the tail.

GAIT

The Chihuahua should move swiftly with a firm, sturdy action with good reach in front equal to the drive from the rear.

The movement of a Chihuahua is called double tracking. The legs converge slightly toward an imaginary center line on the ground. As the dog moves away from you, you should see only the two hind legs. As the Chihuahua moves toward you, you should see only the two front legs.

The appearance of a Chihuahua is of a little dog who is graceful but alert; the expression is saucy and full of life. She is a fast-moving little dog who can keep up with you as you walk along. She should appear to be happy and full of vitality as she trots by your side, with her head and tail up.

TEMPERAMENT

Alert, with terrier-like qualities.

The temperament of the Chihuahua is primarily based on two important factors: inherited traits and proper socialization. For any breed of dog, particularly for dogs as small as the Chihuahua, early socialization outside the family circle is of the utmost importance. If a Chihuahua is kept within the confines of her usual human family and rarely interacts with other people, it is highly unlikely that this size dog will retain her natural friendly disposition. A puppy must be descended from friendly tempered parents and must receive socialization outside her immediate family at a young age, preferably before 8 weeks. If these conditions are met, the puppy should grow up to be friendly and happy with everyone, family and welcomed strangers.

In any event, once you have owned a Chihuahua, you will most likely be a fan of the breed for life.

CHAPTER SEVEN

A Matter of Fact

breeding. People bred for the qualities they desired for certain useful purposes. That's why we have breeds that can track, herd, hunt, guard and go to ground. And that's why there are breeds that are strictly companion animals. The Chihuahua is generally classified in the companion dog division primarily because of his diminutive size, even though he can be trained to do many useful things.

The Chihuahua's ancestry is so steeped in myth, secondhand stories and controversial history that it is almost impossible to separate fact from fiction. The little that was recorded in bygone days was written in archaic Spanish, making later interpretation difficult. Several theories of the Chihuahua's origin are presented

THE CHIHUAHUA'S ANCESTRY

It is said that all dog breeds evolved from only one wild ancestor. Contemporary dog breeds were created and domesticated through selective here because all the fables, legends and stories are fun to read and discuss, even though they may not be true.

MEXICAN ORIGINS

There are those who insist that the Chihuahua is a native Mexican breed because ancient relics of small dog-like creatures were found in the archeological remains of the Mayans, the Toltecs and the Aztecs.

The National Museum in Mexico City houses some interesting sculptures; one is of a small dog with large ears, kissing his master. Another sculpture depicts a woman and child; the woman is carrying a small, erect-eared dog, supposedly a Chihuahua, under one arm.

However, Mayan history is very obscure, and some of these early statues bear little or no resemblance to the modern-day Chihuahua.

Chihuahuas in Toltec Civilization

Sketchy information is available about the Toltec culture, which existed around the ninth century in what is now Mexico. Many believe that the modern-day Chihuahua is a direct

descendant of a dog called the Techichi, depicted in the stone carvings of the monastery of Huejotzingo. The small dogs pictured there bear a striking resemblance to our present-day Chihuahua.

According to a theory that first appeared in print in 1904, the Techichi was crossed with a wild breed called the Perro Chihuahueno. This breed originally lived in the wild mountains of Chihuahua, where it foraged on anything edible. The dogs supposedly lived in holes in the ground; possessed round heads; short, pointed noses; large, erect ears; slender legs and long toenails; and were wild and untrainable.

57

The Chihuahua is generally thought to be of Mexican origin.

WHERE DID DOGS COME FROM?

It can be argued that dogs were right there at man's side from the beginning of time. As soon as human beings began to document their own existence, the dog was among their drawings and inscriptions. Dogs were not just friends, they served a purpose: There were dogs to hunt birds, pull sleds, herd sheep, burrow after rats—even sit in laps! What your dog was originally bred to do influences the way he behaves. The American Kennel Club recognizes over 140 breeds, and there are hundreds more distinct breeds around the world. To make sense of the breeds, they are grouped according to their size or function. The AKC has seven groups:

1) Sporting
2) Working
3) Herding
4) Hounds
5) Terriers
6) Toys
7) Non-Sporting

Can you name a breed from each group? Here's some help: (1) Golden Retriever; (2) Doberman Pinscher; (3) Collie; (4) Beagle; (5) Scottish Terrier; (6) Maltese; and (7) Dalmatian. All modern domestic dogs (*Canis familiaris*) are related, however different they look, and are all descended from *Canis lupus,* the gray wolf.

Chihuahuas in Aztec Culture

The statues from the Aztec era bear an even more striking resemblance to our current dogs. The Aztecs were the conquerors of the Toltecs, and their civilization flourished for several centuries. A small dog was particularly revered by the Aztecs and became the prized possession of the rich. It is said that these little dogs were so treasured by royalty that some families had as many as several hundred specimens. The little dogs supposedly led a life of luxury and were pampered and cared for by slaves; they were even fed a special diet. During that period, the blue Chihuahua was considered especially sacred. Even today, a blue Chihuahua is unusual.

The little dogs were even buried with their wealthy owners because it was believed that the sins of the interred would be transmitted to the dog, thus ensuring a safe resting place for the master. It was also believed that the little dog would see his master safely along the journey through the underworld, guiding the deceased through all kinds of dangerous places in the afterlife.

MEDITERRANEAN ROOTS

Some people believe that the Chihuahua originated in some Mediterranean countries and then became established on the island of Malta. A small dog with the molera trait, common only to the Chihuahua, inhabited that island. From there, the breed was supposed to have been introduced to European countries via trading ships.

Small dogs resembling Chihuahuas can be found in many paintings by European masters. The most noted work is a fresco created by Sondro Botticelli, circa 1482, located in the Sistine Chapel. The painting is one of a series depicting the life of Moses and clearly shows a small, round-headed, smooth-coated little dog with long nails, large eyes and large ears that closely resembles a modern-day Chihuahua. Because this painting was created before Columbus arrived in the New World, it leads one to reconsider the theory that the Chihuahua is a truly Mexican dog.

Because of the evidence in these early European paintings, others believe that the Chihuahua was introduced to Mexico by the Spanish

invaders. However, from the time of the Spanish conquest to the mid-1800s, little is known of the Chihuahua. The Aztecs' magnificent civilization was destroyed by the Spanish invaders, along with all information pertaining to the Chihuahua.

With all these theories, you can pick and choose what to believe about the origin of the Chihuahua.

THE CHIHUAHUA COMES TO THE UNITED STATES

Although it is true that Chihuahua-like remains have been found in some parts of Mexico, the reason many

Chihuahuas were treasured by the Aztecs, and are depicted in statues from that era.

59

people believe the Chihuahua to be of Mexican origin is because it was along the border of Mexico and the United States that the breed became more popular and sought after from the mid-1800s onward. Americans became very interested in the breed around the 1850s.

When the breed was first introduced to the United States, the dogs were not called Chihuahuas. They were usually referred to as Arizona Dogs or Texas Dogs because they were often found along the U.S.-Mexican border. Later, many American tourists, fascinated by these tiny specimens, purchased the dogs from residents of Mexico, and the dogs became known as Mexican

The Chihuahua's distinct ears, large eyes and rounded skull first captivated his many admirers.

Chihuahuas. Chihuahua is the largest northern state of Mexico, where many remains of small dogs resembling the breed were found. Today, the word Mexican has been dropped and the breed is simply called the Chihuahua. In Mexico, the breed is called Chihuahueno.

One of the earliest published articles pertaining to the Chihuahua was written in 1914 by James Watson, an early importer of the breed. In 1888, Watson bought his first Chihuahua for three dollars from a Mexican. The Chihuahua was extremely tiny and did not survive for more than a year. Sometime later, Watson was able to buy several other Chihuahuas from Arizona, Texas and Mexico. He spoke of the Chihuahua as being smart, bright and very affectionate. Watson maintained that unless the dog had a molera in the middle of the top skull, he was not purebred. Basically, the Chihuahuas he describes in his writings are recognizable as the Chihuahuas of today.

SHOW RING HISTORY

In 1884, the first Chihuahua to be exhibited at an American dog show

The American Kennel Club recognizes the Chihuahua as a member of the Toy group.

was classified as a Chihuahua-Terrier and was shown in the Miscellaneous Class. This class was for foreign and unclassified breeds.

One hundred years later, at a show in Philadelphia in November 1984, twenty-six smooth coat Chihuahuas and twenty-five long coat Chihuahuas were in the regular breed classes and five Chihuahuas competed in the Obedience trial.

CHIHUAHUA POPULARITY

The first Chihuahua registered with the AKC was named Midget.

He was born July 18, 1903, and was owned by H. Raynor of El Paso, Texas. There were five registrations of Chihuahuas that year, four in the name of H. Raynor and one registered in the name of J. M. Lee of Los Angeles, also bred by Mr. Raynor.

In 1904, just eleven Chihuahuas were exhibited, but twelve years later, in 1916, fifty Chihuahuas were exhibited at AKC events. By 1967, the popularity of the Chihuahua was increasing rapidly, and that year more than 37,000 Chihuahuas were registered with the AKC. The breed waned in popularity during the 1970s

FAMOUS OWNERS OF CHIHUAHUAS

Billie Holiday

Martina Navratilova

Mickey Rourke

Rosie O'Donnell

Arnold Schwarzenegger

Gertrude Stein

Vincent Price

Madonna

Charo

but is once again on the rise. During the 1990s, it is in the top twenty most popular breeds registered with the AKC.

FAMOUS CHIHUAHUAS

As early as the latter part of the 1800s, Chihuahuas broke into show business. A British performer, Rosina Casselli, had a group of at least a dozen Chihuahuas in her stage act performing all kinds of tricks.

Many people were familiar with the sight of the late Xavier Cugat, noted Latin American bandleader, carrying his Chihuahua with him on stage at each performance. There was even a tale about Mr. Cugat's smuggling his Chihuahua into his hotel room (no dogs were allowed in hotel rooms at that time) by disguising the dog as a baby, complete with bonnet!

General Santa Ana, former president of Mexico, was an enthusiastic Chihuahua owner. Unfortunately, during one of his wartime excursions, his dogs disappeared. To this day, no one has been able to account for the missing Chihuahuas.

Herman Hickman, a huge man and former Yale football coach, owned two tiny 3-pound Chihuahuas named Slugger and Killer.

The fantastic jazz singer, the late Billie Holiday, was a devoted Chihuahua owner, as was the noted singer-actress-comedienne of the 1980s, Christine Ebersole.

Chihuahuas have been depicted in Disney films, television shows, Broadway plays, cartoons, print ads, photographic exhibits, art shows and television series. They have been performers on many late-night talk shows. Chihuahuas make wonderful models because they are easily trained and respond well to direction.

CHIHUAHUAS IN ART

Many famous artists depicted Chihuahuas in their paintings. The National Gallery of Art in Washington, D.C., has a Henri de Toulouse-Lautrec painting entitled *Lady with a Dog*; this painting shows a tiny, smooth-coated Chihuahua-type dog.

Many beautiful paintings can be seen at the headquarters of the AKC in New York City or at the Dog Museum in St. Louis.

Diplomats, athletes and entertainers alike are charmed by the sprightly Chihuahua.

63

CHAPTER EIGHT

On Good Behavior

by Ian Dunbar, Ph.D., MRCVS

Training is the jewel in the crown—the most important aspect of doggy husbandry. There is no more important variable influencing dog behavior and temperament than the dog's education: A well-trained, well-behaved and good-natured puppydog is always a joy to live with, but an untrained and uncivilized dog can be a perpetual nightmare. Moreover, deny the dog an education and she will not have the opportunity to fulfill her own canine potential; neither will she have the ability to communicate effectively with her human companions.

Luckily, modern psychological training methods are easy, efficient, effective and, above all, considerably dog-friendly and user-friendly. Doggy education is as simple as it is enjoyable. But before you can have a good time play-training with your new dog, you have to learn what to do and how to do it. There is no bigger variable influencing the success of dog training than the owner's experience and expertise. Before you embark on the dog's education, you must first educate yourself.

BASIC TRAINING FOR OWNERS

Ideally, basic owner training should begin well before you select your dog. Find out all you can about your chosen breed first, then master rudimentary training and handling skills. If you already have your puppydog, owner training is a dire emergency—the clock is ticking! Especially for puppies, the first few weeks at home are the most important and influential days in the dog's life. Indeed, the cause of most adolescent and adult problems may be traced back to the initial days the pup explores her new home. This is the time to establish the *status quo*—to teach the puppydog how you would like her to behave and so prevent otherwise quite predictable problems.

In addition to consulting breeders and breed books such as this one (which understandably have a positive breed bias), seek out as many pet owners with your breed as you can find. Good points are obvious. What you want to find out are the breed-specific problems, so you can nip

them in the bud. In particular, you should talk to owners with adolescent dogs and make a list of all anticipated problems. Most important, test drive at least half a dozen adolescent and adult dogs of your breed yourself. An 8-week-old puppy is deceptively easy to handle, but she will acquire adult size, speed and strength in just four months, so you should learn now what to prepare for.

Puppy and pet dog training classes offer a convenient venue to locate pet owners and observe dogs in action. For a list of suitable trainers in your area, contact the Association of Pet Dog Trainers (see chapter 9). You may also begin your basic owner training by observing other owners in class. Watch as many classes and test drive as many dogs as possible. Select an upbeat, dog-friendly, people-friendly, fun-and-games, puppydog pet training class to learn the ropes. Also, watch training videos and read training books. You must find out what to do and how to do it *before* you have to do it.

PRINCIPLES OF TRAINING

Most people think training comprises teaching the dog to do things such

65

OWNING A PARTY ANIMAL

It's a fact: The more of the world your puppy is exposed to, the more comfortable she'll be in it. Once your puppy's had her shots, start taking her everywhere with you. Encourage friendly interaction with strangers, expose her to different environments (towns, fields, beaches), and most important, enroll her in a puppy class where she'll get to play with other puppies. These simple, fun, shared activities will develop your pup into a confident socialite, reliable around other people and dogs.

as sit, speak and roll over, but even a 4-week-old pup knows how to do these things already. Instead, the first step in training involves teaching the dog human words for each dog behavior and activity and for each aspect of the dog's environment. That way you, the owner, can more easily participate in the dog's domestic education by directing her to perform specific actions appropriately, that is, at the right time, in the right place and so on. Training opens communication channels, enabling an educated dog to at least understand her owner's requests.

In addition to teaching a dog what we want her to do, it is also necessary to teach her why she should do what we ask. Indeed, 95 percent of training revolves around

The first few weeks at home are the time to teach your puppy how you would like her to behave.

motivating the dog to want to do what we want. Dogs often understand what their owners want; they just don't see the point of doing it— especially when the owner's repetitively boring and seemingly senseless instructions are totally at odds with much more pressing and exciting doggy distractions. It is not so much the dog that is being stubborn or dominant; rather, it is the owner who has failed to acknowledge the dog's needs and feelings and to approach training from the dog's point of view.

The Meaning of Instructions

The secret to successful training is learning how to use training lures to predict or prompt specific behaviors— to coax the dog to do what you want when you want. Any highly valued object (such as a treat or toy) may be used as a lure, which the dog will follow with her eyes and nose. Moving the lure in specific ways entices the dog to move her nose, head and entire body in specific ways. In fact, by learning the art of manipulating various lures, it is possible to teach the dog to assume virtually any body position and perform any action.

FINDING A TRAINER

Have fun with your dog, take a training class! But don't just sign on any dotted line, find a trainer whose approach and style you like and whose students (and their dogs) are really learning. Ask to visit a class to observe a trainer in action. For the names of trainers near you, ask your veterinarian, your pet supply store, your dog-owning neighbors or call (800) PET-DOGS (the Association of Pet Dog Trainers).

Once you have control over the expression of the dog's behaviors and can elicit any body position or behavior at will, you can easily teach the dog to perform on request.

Tell your dog what you want her to do, use a lure to entice her to respond correctly, then profusely praise and maybe reward her once she performs the desired action. For example, verbally request "Fido, sit!" while you move a squeaky toy upwards and backwards over the dog's muzzle (lure-movement and hand signal), smile knowingly as she looks up (to follow the lure) and sits down (as a result of canine anatomical engineering), then praise her to distraction ("Gooood Fido!"). Squeak the toy, offer a training treat

67

and give your dog and yourself a pat on the back.

Being able to elicit desired responses over and over enables the owner to reward the dog over and over. Consequently, the dog begins to think training is fun. For example, the more the dog is rewarded for sitting, the more she enjoys sitting. Eventually the dog comes to realize that, whereas most sitting is appreciated, sitting immediately upon request usually prompts especially enthusiastic praise and a slew of high-level rewards. The dog begins to sit on cue much of the time, showing that she is starting to grasp the meaning of the owner's verbal request and hand signal.

Why Comply?

Most dogs enjoy initial lure-reward training and are only too happy to comply with their owners' wishes. Unfortunately, repetitive drilling without appreciative feedback tends to diminish the dog's enthusiasm until she eventually fails to see the point of complying anymore. Moreover, as the dog approaches adolescence she becomes more easily distracted as she develops other interests. Lengthy sessions with repetitive exercises tend to bore and demotivate both parties. If it's not fun, the owner doesn't do it and neither does the dog.

Integrate training into your dog's life: The greater number of training sessions each day and the shorter they are, the more willingly compliant your dog will become. Make sure to have a short (just a few seconds) training interlude before every enjoyable canine activity. For example, ask your dog to sit to greet people, to sit before you throw her Frisbee and to sit for her supper. Really, sitting is no different from a canine "Please." Also, include numerous short training interludes during every enjoyable canine pastime, for example, when playing with the dog or when she is running in the park. In this fashion, doggy distractions may be effectively converted into rewards for training. Just as all games have rules, fun becomes training . . . and training becomes fun.

Eventually, rewards actually become unnecessary to continue motivating your dog. If trained with consideration and kindness, performing the desired behaviors will become self-rewarding and, in a sense, your dog will motivate herself. Just as it is not necessary to reward a

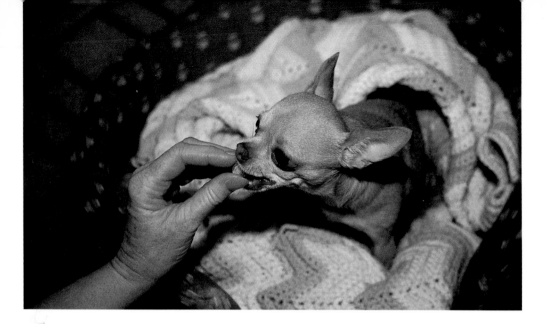

human companion during an enjoyable walk in the park, or following a game of tennis, it is hardly necessary to reward our best friend—the dog—for walking by our side or while playing fetch. Human company during enjoyable activities is reward enough for most dogs.

Even though your dog has become self-motivating, it's still good to praise and pet her a lot and offer rewards once in a while, especially for a job well done. And if for no other reason, praising and rewarding others is good for the human heart.

Punishment

Without a doubt, lure-reward training is by far the best way to teach:

Entice your dog to do what you want and then reward her for doing so. Unfortunately, a human shortcoming is to take the good for granted and to moan and groan at the bad. Specifically, the dog's many good behaviors are ignored while the owner focuses on punishing the dog for making mistakes. In extreme cases, instruction is limited to punishing mistakes made by a trainee dog, child, employee or husband, even though it has been proven punishment training is notoriously inefficient and ineffective and is decidedly unfriendly and combative. It teaches the dog that training is a drag, almost as quickly as it teaches the dog to dislike her trainer. Why treat our best friends like our worst enemies?

The greater number of training sessions each day and the shorter they are, the more willingly compliant your dog will become.

Punishment training is laborious and time-consuming. Using positive reinforcement to train your Chihuahua is much more effective.

Punishment training is also much more laborious and time-consuming. Whereas it takes only a finite amount of time to teach a dog what to chew, for example, it takes much, much longer to punish the dog for each and every mistake. Remember, there is only one right way! So why not teach that right way from the outset?!

To make matters worse, punishment training causes severe lapses in the dog's reliability. Since it is obviously impossible to punish the dog each and every time she misbehaves, the dog quickly learns to distinguish between those times when she must comply (so as to avoid impending punishment) and those times when

she need not comply because punishment is impossible. Such times include when the dog is off leash and 6 feet away, when the owner is otherwise engaged (talking to a friend, watching television, taking a shower, tending to the baby or chatting on the telephone) or when the dog is left at home alone.

Instances of misbehavior will be numerous when the owner is away, because even when the dog complied in the owner's looming presence, she did so unwillingly. The dog was forced to act against her will, rather than molding her will to want to please. Hence, when the owner is absent, not only does the dog know

Using a favorite toy as a lure/ reward is one of the most effective tools for training.

she need not comply, she simply does not want to. Again, the trainee is not a stubborn vindictive beast, but rather the trainer has failed to teach. Punishment training invariably creates unpredictable Jekyll and Hyde behavior.

TRAINER'S TOOLS

Many training books extol the virtues of a vast array of training paraphernalia and electronic and metallic gizmos, most of which are designed for canine restraint, correction and punishment, rather than for actual facilitation of doggy education. In reality, most effective training tools are not found in stores; they come from within ourselves. In addition to a willing dog, all you really need is a functional human brain, gentle hands, a loving heart and a good attitude.

In terms of equipment, all dogs do require a quality buckle collar to sport dog tags and to attach the leash (for safety and to comply with local leash laws). Hollow chew toys (like Kongs or sterilized longbones) and a dog bed or collapsible crate are musts for housetraining. Three additional tools are required:

1. specific lures (training treats and toys) to predict and prompt specific desired behaviors;

2. rewards (praise, affection, training treats and toys) to reinforce for the dog what a lot of fun it all is; and

3. knowledge—how to convert the dog's favorite activities and games (potential distractions to training) into "life-rewards," which may be employed to facilitate training.

The most powerful of these is knowledge. Education is the key! Watch training classes, participate in training classes, watch videos, read books, enjoy play-training with your dog and then your dog will say "Please," and your dog will say "Thank you!"

HOUSETRAINING

If dogs were left to their own devices, certainly they would chew, dig and bark for entertainment and then no doubt highlight a few areas of their living space with sprinkles of urine, in much the same way we decorate by hanging pictures. Consequently, when we ask a dog to live with us, we must teach her *where* she may dig, *where* she may perform her toilet duties, *what* she may chew and *when* she may bark. After all, when left at home alone for many hours, we cannot expect the dog to amuse herself by completing crosswords or watching TV!

Education and guidance are important when establishing rules for your Chihuahua to follow.

Also, it would be decidedly unfair to keep the house rules a secret from the dog, and then get angry and punish the poor critter for inevitably transgressing rules she did not even know existed. Remember: Without adequate education and guidance, the dog will be forced to establish her own rules—doggy rules—and most probably will be at odds with the owner's view of domestic living.

Since most problems develop during the first few days the dog is at home, prospective dog owners must be certain they are quite clear about the principles of housetraining *before* they get a dog. Early misbehaviors quickly become established as the *status quo*—becoming firmly entrenched as hard-to-break bad habits, which set the precedent for years to come. Make sure to teach your dog good habits right from the start. Good habits are just as hard to break as bad ones!

Ideally, when a new dog comes home, try to arrange for someone to be present as much as possible during the first few days (for adult dogs) or weeks for puppies. With only a little forethought, it is surprisingly easy to find a puppy sitter, such as a retired person, who would be willing to eat from your refrigerator and

HOUSETRAINING 1-2-3

1. **Prevent Mistakes.** When you can't supervise your puppy, confine her in a single room or in her crate (but don't leave her for too long!). Puppy-proof the area by laying down newspapers so that if she does make a mistake it won't matter.

2. **Teach Where.** Take your puppy to the spot you want her to use every hour.

3. **Control When.** When she goes, praise her profusely and give her three favorite treats.

watch your television while keeping an eye on the newcomer to encourage the dog to play with chew toys and to ensure she goes outside on a regular basis.

Potty Training

Follow these steps to teach the dog where she should relieve herself:

1. never let her make a single mistake;

2. let her know where you want her to go; and

3. handsomely reward her for doing so: "GOOOOOOOD DOG!!!" liver treat, liver treat, liver treat!

Preventing Mistakes

A single mistake is a training disaster, since it heralds many more in future weeks. And each time the dog soils the house, this further reinforces the dog's unfortunate preference for an indoor, carpeted toilet. Do not let an unhousetrained dog have full run of the house.

When you are away from home, or cannot pay full attention, confine the dog to an area where elimination is appropriate, such as an outdoor run or, better still, a small, comfortable indoor kennel with access to an outdoor run. When confined in this manner, most dogs will naturally housetrain themselves.

If that's not possible, confine the dog to an area, such as a utility room, kitchen, basement or garage, where elimination may not be desired in the long run but as an interim measure

Short-term close confinement strongly inhibits urination and defecation, since the dog doesn't want to soil her sleeping area.

it is certainly preferable to doing it all around the house. Use newspaper to cover the floor of the dog's day room. The newspaper may be used to soak up the urine and to wrap up and dispose of the feces. Once your dog develops a preferred spot for eliminating, it is only necessary to cover that part of the floor with newspaper. The smaller papered area may then be moved (only a little each day) towards the door to the outside. Thus the dog will develop the tendency to go to the door when she needs to relieve herself.

Never confine an unhousetrained dog to a crate for long periods. Doing so would force the dog to soil the crate and ruin its usefulness as an aid for housetraining (see the following discussion).

Teaching Where

In order to teach your dog where you would like her to do her business, you have to be there to direct the proceedings—an obvious, yet often neglected, fact of life. In order to be there to teach the dog where to go, you need to know *when* she needs to go. Indeed, the success of housetraining depends on the owner's ability to predict these times. Certainly, a regular feeding schedule will facilitate

prediction somewhat, but there is nothing like "loading the deck" and influencing the timing of the outcome yourself!

Whenever you are at home, make sure the dog is under constant supervision and/or confined to a small area. If already well trained, simply instruct the dog to lie down in her bed or basket. Alternatively, confine the dog to a crate (doggy den) or tiedown (a short, 18-inch lead that can be clipped to an eye hook in the baseboard near her bed). Short-term close confinement strongly inhibits urination and defecation, since the dog does not want to soil her sleeping area. Thus, when you release the puppydog each hour, she will definitely need to urinate immediately and defecate every third or fourth hour. Keep the dog confined to her doggy den and take her to her intended toilet area each hour, every hour and on the hour. When taking your dog outside, instruct her to sit quietly before opening the door— she will soon learn to sit by the door when she needs to go out!

Teaching Why

Being able to predict when the dog needs to go enables the owner to be

75

on the spot to praise and reward the dog. Each hour, hurry the dog to the intended toilet area in the yard, issue the appropriate instruction ("Go pee!" or "Go poop!"), then give the dog three to four minutes to produce. Praise and offer a couple of training treats when successful. The treats are important because many people fail to praise their dogs with feeling . . . and housetraining is hardly the time for understatement. So either loosen up and enthusiastically praise that dog: "Wuzzzer-wuzzer-wuzzer, hoooser good wuffer den? Hoooo went pee for Daddy?" Or say "Good dog!" as best you can and offer the treats for effect.

Following elimination is an ideal time for a spot of play-training in the yard or house. Also, an empty dog may be allowed greater freedom around the house for the next half . hour or so, just as long as you keep an eye out to make sure she does not get into other kinds of mischief. If you are preoccupied and cannot pay full attention, confine the dog to her doggy den once more to enjoy a peaceful snooze or to play with her many chew toys.

If your dog does not eliminate within the allotted time outside— no biggie! Back to her doggy den, and then try again after another hour.

As I own large dogs, I always feel more relaxed walking an empty dog, knowing that I will not need to finish our stroll weighted down with bags of feces!

Beware of falling into the trap of walking the dog to get her to eliminate. The good ol' dog walk is such an enormous highlight in the dog's life that it represents the single biggest potential reward in domestic dogdom. However, when in a hurry, or during inclement weather, many owners abruptly terminate the walk the moment the dog has done her business. This, in effect, severely punishes the dog for doing the right thing, in the right place at the right time. Consequently, many dogs become strongly inhibited from eliminating outdoors because they know it will signal an abrupt end to an otherwise thoroughly enjoyable walk.

Instead, instruct the dog to relieve herself in the yard prior to going for a walk. If you follow the above instructions, most dogs soon learn to eliminate on cue. As soon as the dog eliminates, praise (and offer a treat or two)—"Good dog! Let's go walkies!" Use the walk as a reward for eliminating in the yard. If the dog does not go, put her back in her doggy den and think about a walk later on. You will find with a "No feces—no walk" policy, your dog will become one of the fastest defecators in the business.

If you do not have a backyard, instruct the dog to eliminate right outside your front door prior to the walk. Not only will this facilitate cleanup and disposal of the feces in your own trash can, but, also, the walk may again be used as a colossal reward.

CHEWING AND BARKING

Short-term close confinement also teaches the dog that occasional quiet moments are a reality of domestic living. Your puppydog is extremely impressionable during her first few weeks at home. Regular confinement at this time soon exerts a calming influence over the dog's personality. Remember, once the dog is house-trained and calmer, there will be a whole lifetime ahead for the dog to enjoy full run of the house and gar-den. On the other hand, by letting the newcomer have unrestricted ac-cess to the entire household and al-lowing her to run willy-nilly, she will most certainly develop a bunch of

behavior problems in short order, no doubt necessitating confinement later in life. It would not be fair to remedially restrain and confine a dog you have trained, through neglect, to run free.

When confining the dog, make sure she always has an impressive array of suitable chew toys. Kongs and sterilized longbones (both readily available from pet stores) make the best chew toys, since they are hol-low and may be stuffed with treats to heighten the dog's interest. For example, by stuffing the little hole at the top of a Kong with a small piece of freeze-dried liver, the dog will not want to leave it alone.

TOYS THAT EARN THEIR KEEP

To entertain even the most distracted of dogs, while you're home or away, have a selection of the following toys on hand: hollow chew toys (like Kongs, sterilized hollow longbones and cubes or balls that can be stuffed with kib-ble). Smear peanut butter or honey on the in-side of the hollow toy or bone, and stuff the bone with kibble and your dog will think of nothing else but working the object to get at the food. Great to take your dog's mind off the fact that you've left the house.

Remember, treats do not have to be junk food and they certainly should not represent extra calories. Rather, treats should be part of each dog's regular daily diet: Some food may be served in the dog's bowl for breakfast and dinner, some food may be used as training treats, and some food may be used for stuffing chew toys. I regularly stuff my dogs' many Kongs with different shaped biscuits and kibble. The kibble seems to fall out fairly easily, as do the oval-shaped biscuits, thus rewarding the dog instantaneously for checking out the chew toys. The bone-shaped biscuits fall out after a while, rewarding the dog for worrying at the chew toy. But the triangular biscuits never come out. They remain inside the Kong as lures, maintaining the dog's fascination with her chew toy. To further focus the dog's interest, I always make sure to flavor the triangular biscuits by rubbing them with a little cheese or freeze-dried liver.

If stuffed chew toys are reserved especially for times the dog is confined, the puppydog will soon learn to enjoy quiet moments in her doggy den and she will quickly develop a chew-toy habit—a good habit! This is a simple autoshaping process; all the owner has to do is set up the situation and the dog all but trains herself—easy and effective. Even when the dog is given run of the house, her first inclination will be to indulge her rewarding chew-toy habit rather than destroy less-attractive household articles, such as curtains, carpets, chairs and compact disks. Similarly, a chew-toy chewer will be less inclined to scratch and chew herself excessively. Also, if the dog busies herself as a recreational chewer, she will be less inclined to develop into a recreational barker or digger when left at home alone.

Stuff a number of chew toys whenever the dog is left confined and remove the extra-special-tasting treats when you return. Your dog will now amuse herself with her chew toys before falling asleep and then resume playing with her chew toys when she expects you to return. Since most owner-absent misbehavior happens right after you leave and right before your expected return, your puppydog will now be conveniently preoccupied with her chew toys at these times.

COME AND SIT

Most puppies will happily approach virtually anyone, whether called or

78

not; that is, until they collide with adolescence and develop other more important doggy interests, such as sniffing a multiplicity of exquisite odors on the grass. Your mission, Mr./Ms. Owner, is to teach and reward the pup for coming reliably, willingly and happily when called— and you have just three months to get it done. Unless adequately reinforced, your puppy's tendency to approach people will self-destruct by adolescence.

Call your dog ("Fido, come!"), open your arms (and maybe squat down) as a welcoming signal, waggle a treat or toy as a lure and reward the puppydog when she comes running. Do not wait to praise the dog until she reaches you—she may come 95 percent of the way and then run off after some distraction. Instead, praise the dog's first step towards you and continue praising enthusiastically for every step she takes in your direction.

When the rapidly approaching puppydog is three lengths away from impact, instruct her to sit ("Fido, sit!") and hold the lure in front of you in an outstretched hand. As Fido decelerates to nose the lure, move the treat upwards and backwards just over her muzzle with an upwards motion of your extended

Your puppy is impressionable during her first few weeks at home.

arm (palm-upwards). As the dog looks up to follow the lure, she will sit down (if she jumps up, you are holding the lure too high). Praise the dog for sitting. Move backwards and call her again. Repeat this many times over, always praising when Fido comes and sits; on occasion, reward her.

For the first couple of trials, use a training treat both as a lure to entice the dog to come and sit and as a reward for doing so. Thereafter, try to use different items as lures and rewards. For example, lure the dog with a Kong or Frisbee but reward her with a food treat. Or lure the dog with a food treat but pat her and throw a tennis ball as a reward. After just a few repetitions, dispense with the lures and rewards; the dog will begin to respond willingly to your verbal requests and hand signals just for the prospect of praise from your heart and affection from your hands.

Instruct every family member, friend and visitor how to get the dog to come and sit. Invite people over for a series of pooch parties; do not keep the pup a secret—let other people enjoy this puppy, and let the pup enjoy other people. Puppydog parties are not only fun, they easily attract a lot of people to help you train your dog. Send out those invitations for puppy parties and teach your dog to be mannerly and socially acceptable.

Even though your dog quickly masters obedient recalls in the house, her reliability may falter when playing in the backyard or local park. Ironically, it is the owner who has unintentionally trained the dog not to respond in these instances. By allowing the dog to play and run around and otherwise have a good time, but then to call the dog to put her on leash to take her home, the dog quickly learns playing is fun but training is a drag. Thus, playing in the park becomes a severe distraction, which works against training. Bad news!

Instead, whether playing with the dog off leash or on leash, request her to come at frequent intervals—say, every minute or so. On most occasions, praise and pet the dog for a few seconds while she is sitting, then tell her to go play again. For especially fast recalls, offer a couple of training treats and take the time to praise and pet the dog enthusiastically before releasing her. The dog will learn that coming when called is not necessarily the end of the play session, and neither is it the end of the world; rather, it signals an enjoyable, quality time-out with the owner before resuming play once more. In fact, playing in the park now becomes a very effective life-reward, which works to facilitate training by reinforcing each obedient and timely recall. Good news!

SIT, DOWN, STAND AND ROLLOVER

Teaching the dog a variety of body positions is easy for owner and dog, impressive for spectators and extremely useful for all. Using lure-reward techniques, it is possible to train several positions at once to verbal commands or hand signals (which impress the socks off onlookers).

Sit and down—the two control commands—prevent or resolve nearly a hundred behavior problems. For example, if the dog happily and obediently sits or lies down when requested, she cannot jump on visitors, dash out the front door, run around and chase her tail, pester other dogs, harass cats or annoy family, friends or strangers. Additionally, "Sit" or "Down" are the best emergency commands for off-leash control.

It is easier to teach and maintain a reliable sit than maintain a reliable recall. Sit is the purest and simplest of commands—either the dog is sitting or she is not. If there is any change of circumstances or potential danger in the park, for example, simply instruct the dog to sit. If she sits, you have a number of options: Allow the dog to resume playing when she is safe, walk up and put the dog on leash or call the dog. The dog will be much more likely to come when called if she has already acknowledged her compliance by sitting. If

Your dog will quickly learn that the appearance of a leash means the arrival of a long-awaited trip outdoors.

81

the dog does not sit in the park—train her to!

Stand and rollover-stay are the two positions for examining the dog. Your veterinarian will love you to distraction if you take a little time to teach the dog to stand still and roll over and play possum. Also, your vet bills will be smaller because it will take the veterinarian less time to examine your dog. The rollover-stay is an especially useful command and is really just a variation of the downstay: Whereas the dog lies prone in

Chihuahuas, like all dogs, will need to have their abundant energy and curiosity reined in by efficient training.

the traditional down, she lies supine in the rollover-stay.

As with teaching come and sit, the training techniques to teach the dog to assume all other body positions on cue are user-friendly and dog-friendly. Simply give the appropriate request, lure the dog into the desired body position using a training treat or toy and then praise (and maybe reward) the dog as soon as she complies. Try not to touch the dog to get her to respond. If you teach the dog by guiding her into

position, the dog will quickly learn that rump-pressure means sit, for example, but as yet you still have no control over your dog if she is just 6 feet away. It will still be necessary to teach the dog to sit on request. So do not make training a time-consuming two-step process; instead, teach the dog to sit to a verbal request or hand signal from the outset. Once the dog sits willingly when requested, by all means use your hands to pet the dog when she does so.

To teach down when the dog is already sitting, say "Fido, down!" Hold the lure in one hand (palm down) and lower that hand to the floor between the dog's forepaws. As the dog lowers her head to follow the lure, slowly move the lure away from the dog just a fraction (in front of her paws). The dog will lie down as she stretches her nose forward to follow the lure. Praise the dog when she does so. If the dog stands up, you pulled the lure away too far and too quickly.

When teaching the dog to lie down from the standing position, say "Down" and lower the lure to the floor as before. Once the dog has lowered her forequarters and assumed a play bow, gently and slowly move the lure towards the dog between her forelegs. Praise the dog as soon as her rear end plops down.

After just a couple of trials it will be possible to alternate sits and downs and have the dog energetically perform doggy push-ups. Praise the dog a lot, and after half a dozen or so push-ups reward the dog with a training treat or toy. You will notice the more energetically you move your arm—upwards (palm up) to get the dog to sit, and downwards (palm down) to get the

dog to lie down—the more energetically the dog responds to your requests. Now try training the dog in silence and you will notice she has also learned to respond to hand signals. Yeah! Not too shabby for the first session.

To teach stand from the sitting position, say "Fido, stand," slowly move the lure half a dog-length away from the dog's nose, keeping it at nose level, and praise the dog as she stands to follow the lure. As soon as the dog stands, lower the lure to just beneath the dog's chin to entice her to look down; otherwise she will stand and then sit immediately. To prompt the dog to stand from the down position, move the lure half a dog-length upwards and away from the dog, holding the lure at standing nose height from the floor.

Teaching rollover is best started from the down position, with the dog lying on one side, or at least with both hind legs stretched out on the same side. Say "Fido, bang!" and move the lure backwards and alongside the dog's muzzle to her elbow (on the side of her outstretched hind legs). Once the dog looks to the side and backwards, very slowly move the lure upwards to the dog's shoulder and backbone. Tickling the dog in

To get your puppy used to the feel of a leash, put her on it for a few short trips around the house.

bang!" and give the appropriate hand signal (with index finger pointed and thumb cocked in true Sam Spade fashion), then in one fluid movement lure her to first lie down and then rollover-stay as above.

Teaching the dog to stay in each of the above four positions becomes a piece of cake after first teaching the dog not to worry at the toy or treat training lure. This is best accomplished by hand feeding dinner kibble. Hold a piece of kibble firmly in your hand and softly instruct "Off!" Ignore any licking and slobbering for however long the dog worries at the treat, but say "Take it!" and offer the kibble the instant the dog breaks contact with her muzzle. Repeat this a few times, and then up the ante and insist the dog remove her muzzle for one whole second before offering the kibble. Then progressively refine your criteria and have the dog not touch your hand (or treat) for longer and longer periods on each trial, such as for two seconds, four seconds, then six, ten, fifteen, twenty, thirty seconds and so on.

The dog soon learns: (1) worrying at the treat never gets results, whereas (2) noncontact is often rewarded after a variable time lapse.

the goolies (groin area) often invokes a reflex-raising of the hind leg as an appeasement gesture, which facilitates the tendency to roll over. If you move the lure too quickly and the dog jumps into the standing position, have patience and start again. As soon as the dog rolls onto her back, keep the lure stationary and mesmerize the dog with a relaxing tummy rub.

To teach rollover-stay when the dog is standing or moving, say "Fido,

Teaching "Off!" has many useful applications in its own right. Additionally, instructing the dog not to touch a training lure often produces spontaneous and magical stays. Request the dog to stand-stay, for example, and not to touch the lure. At first set your sights on a short two-second stay before rewarding the dog. (Remember, every long journey begins with a single step.) However, on subsequent trials, gradually and progressively increase the length of stay required to receive a reward. In no time at all your dog will stand calmly for a minute or so.

RELEVANCY TRAINING

Once you have taught the dog what you expect her to do when requested to come, sit, lie down, stand, rollover and stay, the time is right to teach the dog why she should comply with your wishes. The secret is to have many (many) extremely short training interludes (two to five seconds each) at numerous (numerous) times during the course of the dog's day. Especially work with the dog immediately before the dog's good times and during the dog's good times. For example, ask your dog to sit and/or

lie down each time before opening doors, serving meals, offering treats and tummy rubs; ask the dog to perform a few controlled doggy push-ups before letting her off leash or throwing a tennis ball; and perhaps request the dog to sit-down-sit-stand-down-stand-rollover before inviting her to cuddle on the couch.

Similarly, request the dog to sit many times during play or on walks, and in no time at all the dog will be only too pleased to follow your instructions because she has learned that a compliant response heralds all sorts of goodies. Basically all you are trying to teach the dog is how to say please: "Please throw the tennis ball. Please may I snuggle on the couch."

Remember, it is important to keep training interludes short and to have many short sessions each and every day. The shortest (and most useful) session comprises asking the dog to sit and then go play during a play session. When trained this way, your dog will soon associate training with good times. In fact, the dog may be unable to distinguish between training and good times and, indeed, there should be no distinction. The warped concept that training involves forcing the dog to comply and/or

85

dominating her will is totally at odds with the picture of a truly well-trained dog. In reality, enjoying a game of training with a dog is no different from enjoying a game of backgammon or tennis with a friend; and walking with a dog should be no different from strolling with a spouse, or with buddies on the golf course.

CHAPTER NINE

Resources

BOOKS

About Chihuahuas

Pisano, Beverly. *Chihuahuas*. Neptune, N.J.: T.F.H. Publications, 1988.

Terry, E. Ruth. *The New Chihuahua*. New York: Howell Book House, 1990.

About Health Care

American Kennel Club. *American Kennel Club Dog Care and Training*. New York: Howell Book House, 1991.

Carlson, Delbert, DVM, and James Giffen, MD. *Dog Owner's Home Veterinary Handbook*. New York: Howell Book House, 1992.

DeBitetto, James, DVM, and Sarah Hodgson. *You & Your Puppy*. New York: Howell Book House, 1995.

Lane, Marion. *The Humane Society of the United States Complete Guide to Dog Care*. New York: Little, Brown & Co., 1998.

McGinnis, Terri. *The Well Dog Book*. New York: Random House, 1991.

Schwartz, Stephanie, DVM. *First Aid for Dogs: An Owner's Guide to a Happy Healthy Pet*. New York: Howell Book House, 1998.

Volhard, Wendy and Kerry L. Brown. *The Holistic Guide for a Healthy Dog*. New York: Howell Book House, 1995.

About Training

Ammen, Amy. *Training in No Time*. New York: Howell Book House, 1995.

Benjamin, Carol Lea. *Mother Knows Best*. New York: Howell Book House, 1985.

Bohnenkamp, Gwen. *Manners for the Modern Dog*. San Francisco: Perfect Paws, 1990.

Dunbar, Ian, Ph.D., MRCVS. *Dr. Dunbar's Good Little Book*. James & Kenneth Publishers, 2140 Shattuck Ave. #2406, Berkeley, CA 94704. (510) 658-8588. Order from Publisher.

Evans, Job Michael. *People, Pooches and Problems.* New York: Howell Book House, 1991.

Palika, Liz. *All Dogs Need Some Training.* New York: Howell Book House, 1997.

Volhard, Jack and Melissa Bartlett. *What All Good Dogs Should Know: The Sensible Way to Train.* New York: Howell Book House, 1991.

About Activities

Hall, Lynn. *Dog Showing for Beginners.* New York: Howell Book House, 1994.

O'Neil, Jackie. *All About Agility.* New York: Howell Book House, 1998.

Simmons-Moake, Jane. *Agility Training, The Fun Sport for All Dogs.* New York: Howell Book House, 1991.

Vanacore, Connie. *Dog Showing: An Owner's Guide.* New York: Howell Book House, 1990.

Volhard, Jack and Wendy. *The Canine Good Citizen.* New York: Howell Book House, 1994.

MAGAZINES

THE AKC GAZETTE, The Official Journal for the Sport of Purebred Dogs
American Kennel Club
260 Madison Ave.
New York, NY 10016
www.akc.org

DOG FANCY
Fancy Publications
3 Burroughs
Irvine, CA 92618
(714) 855-8822
http://dogfancy.com

DOG WORLD
Maclean Hunter Publishing Corp.
500 N. Dearborn, Ste. 1100
Chicago, IL 60610
(312) 396-0600
www.dogworldmag.com

PETLIFE: Your Companion Animal Magazine
Magnolia Media Group
1400 Two Tandy Center
Fort Worth, TX 76102
(800) 767-9377
www.petlifeweb.com

DOG & KENNEL
7-L Dundas Circle
Greensboro, NC 27407
(336) 292-4047
www.dogandkennel.com

MORE INFORMATION ABOUT CHIHUAHUAS

National Breed Club

CHIHUAHUA CLUB OF AMERICA
Corresponding Secretary:
Diana Garren
16 Hillgirt Rd.
Hendersonville, NC 28792

Breeder Contact:
Josephine DeMenna
2 Maple St.
Wilton, CT 06897

Breed Rescue:
Chihuahua Club of America
Sharon Hermosillo
(408) 251-6470

The Club can send you information on all aspects of the breed including the names and addresses of breed clubs in your area, as well as obedience clubs. Inquire about membership.

The American Kennel Club

The American Kennel Club (AKC), devoted to the advancement of purebred dogs, is the oldest and largest registry organization in this country. Every breed recognized by the AKC has a national (parent) club. National clubs are a great source of information on your breed. The affiliated clubs hold AKC events and use AKC rules to hold performance events, dog shows, educational programs, health clinics and training classes. The AKC staff is divided between offices in New York City and Raleigh, North Carolina. The AKC has an excellent web site that provides information on the organization and all AKC-recognized breeds. The address is **www.akc.org.**

For registration and performance events information, or for customer service, contact:

THE AMERICAN KENNEL CLUB
5580 Centerview Dr., Suite 200
Raleigh, NC 27606
(919) 233-9767

The AKC's executive offices and the AKC Library (open to the public) are at this address:

THE AMERICAN KENNEL CLUB
260 Madison Ave.
New York, New York 10014
(212) 696-8200 (general information)
(212) 696-8246 (AKC Library)
www.akc.org

UNITED KENNEL CLUB
100 E. Kilgore Rd.
Kalamazoo, MI 49001-5598
(616) 343-9020
www.ukcdogs.com

AMERICAN RARE BREED ASSOCIATION
9921 Frank Tippett Rd.
Cheltenham, MD 20623
(301) 868-5718 (voice or fax)
www.arba.org

CANADIAN KENNEL CLUB
89 Skyway Ave., Ste. 100
Etobicoke, Ontario
Canada M9W 6R4
(416) 675-5511
www.ckc.ca

ORTHOPEDIC FOUNDATION FOR ANIMALS (OFA)
2300 E. Nifong Blvd.
Columbia, MO 65201-3856
(314) 442-0418
www.offa.org/

Trainers

Animal Behavior & Training Associates (ABTA)
9018 Balboa Blvd., Ste. 591
Northridge, CA 91325
(800) 795-3294
www.Good-dawg.com

Association of Pet Dog Trainers (APDT)
(800) PET-DOGS
www.apdt.com

89

National Association of Dog Obedience Instructors (NADOI)
729 Grapevine Highway, Ste. 369
Hurst, TX 76054-2085
www.kimberly.uidaho.edu/nadoi

Associations

Delta Society
P.O. Box 1080
Renton, WA 98507-1080
(Promotes the human/animal bond through pet-assisted therapy and other programs)
www.petsform.com/DELTASOCIETY/dsi400.htm

Dog Writers Association of America (DWAA)
Sally Cooper, Secretary
222 Woodchuck Lane
Harwinton, CT 06791
www.dwaa.org

National Association for Search and Rescue (NASAR)
4500 Southgate Place, Ste. 100
Chantilly, VA 20157
(703) 222-6277
www.nasar.org

Therapy Dogs International
6 Hilltop Rd.
Mendham, NJ 07945

OTHER USEFUL RESOURCES— WEB SITES

General Information— Links to Additional Sites, On-Line Shopping

www.k9web.com – resources for the dog world

www.netpet.com – pet related products, software and services

www.apapets.com – The American Pet Association

www.dogandcatbooks.com – book catalog

www.dogbooks.com – on-line bookshop

www.animal.discovery.com/ – cable television channel on-line

Health

www.avma.org – American Veterinary Medical Association (AVMA)

www.avma.org/care4pets/avmaloss.htm – AVMA site dedicated to consideration of euthanizing sick pets and the grieving process after losing a pet.

www.aplb.org – Association for Pet Loss Bereavement (APLB)—contains an index of national hot lines for on-line and office counseling.

www.netfopets.com/AskTheExperts.html – veterinary questions answered on-line.

Breed Information

www.bestdogs.com/news/ – newsgroup

www.cheta.net/connect/canine/breeds/ – Canine Connections Breed Information Index

91